UPSELLING TECHNIQUES

(That Really Work!)

Stephan Schiffman

Adams Media
Avon, Massachusetts

To the memory of my mother, Martha F. Schiffman

Published by Adams Media, an F+W Publications Company
57 Littlefield Street, Avon, MA 02322
www.adamsmedia.com

ISBN: 1-59337-273-6

Printed in Canada.

J I H G F E D C B A

Library of Congress Cataloging-in-Publication Data
Schiffman, Stephan.
Upselling techniques (that really work!) / Stephan Schiffman.
p. cm.
ISBN 1-59337-273-6
1. Selling. I. Title.
HF5438.25.S3347 2005
658.85—dc22
2004025949

This publication is designed to provide accurate and authoritative information
with regard to the subject matter covered. It is sold with the understanding that
the publisher is not engaged in rendering legal, accounting, or other professional
advice. If legal advice or other expert assistance is required, the services of a
competent professional person should be sought.
  —From a *Declaration of Principles* jointly adopted by a Committee of the
American Bar Association and a Committee of Publishers and Associations

Many of the designations used by manufacturers and sellers to distinguish their
products are claimed as trademarks. Where those designations appear in this
book and Adams Media was aware of a trademark claim, the designations have
been printed with initial capital letters.

This book is available at quantity discounts for bulk purchases.
For information, please call 1-800-872-5627.

Acknowledgments

Grateful appreciation goes out to all those who helped make this book a reality, especially Brandon Toropov, Steve Bookbinder, Danielle Chiotti, Gary Krebs, Stephanie Kip Rostan, Daniel Greenberg, Michele Reisner, Amy Stagg, Lynne Einleger, Martha Rios, Scott Forman, Alan Koval, Surendra Sewsankar, David Rivera, Kara Maloney, Carlos Alvarez, and David Toropov.

Contents

Part I: Foundation Concepts

  How to take the initiative in conversations with prospects while building the foundations of an effective selling strategy.

  Upselling defined—the process, the challenges, and the great results.

  What kinds of questions you should—and shouldn't—ask to promote upselling.

  Why "less is more" applies to upselling and how to move the process forward during nonsales conversations.

  The three words that determine every buying decision and that form the basis of the most effective closing strategy.

  How to effectively incorporate this essential substep into the sales process.

  Gathering the information that makes a successful presentation possible.

  Ways to move past the inevitable obstacles raised by these critical topics.

  Fifteen principles that every successful upseller will follow.

| Contents |

Contents

Author's Note

It has been nearly two decades since the release of the first edition of my first book, *Cold Calling Techniques (That Really Work!)*. In that time, the economy has changed, my business has changed, and the sales training industry has changed. I've learned a lot. And I think this book, which covers the back end of the sales process in the same way my first book covered the front end of that process, is a necessary addition to the literature. I was amazed at how little had been published on this important subject, and how much practical firsthand experience we had on tap at D.E.I. Management Group when the time came to develop the manuscript.

As always, I'm eager to hear what you think of the chapters that follow. Please contact me and let me know your thoughts and feedback.

Stephan Schiffman
contactus@dei-sales.com
New York City
February 2005

A Tale of Two Conversations

You will find the key to success under the alarm clock.
—BENJAMIN FRANKLIN

I WALKED INTO A RADIO SHACK the other morning to buy a calculator. The lady there said to me as I stood at the counter with my purchase, "You know, we've got this great sale on batteries today. They're only a dollar ninety-nine for a four-pack."

When she said this, she was fully engaged in the conversation. She made eye contact with me, she smiled at me as she rang up my purchase, and then she said her piece.

Here's my question: If she says that to 100 people, do you think 10 of them might decide to throw a package of batteries onto the purchase total? If she did that every day, what do you think the outcome would be for her store? If every Radio Shack store did that for an entire year, what do you think the results of the effort would be, and how do you think the effort would play out across the chain?

By contrast, later that same day, I went into a hardware store and asked the clerk, "Hey, how much is this?" I held up a snazzy carpenter's level. The guy checks his book, looks up for a split second, and says, "Thirty-nine ninety-eight." And then went back to his business.

That's all he said: "Thirty-nine ninety-eight."

Which of these two conversations . . . which of these two guiding philosophies . . . is driving your organization's upselling efforts?

In this book, you will learn how to have more money-generating conversations, in more situations, than you're having now (along the lines of the lady at Radio Shack). You will also learn how to avoid dead-end, low-revenue conversations (like the one the guy at the hardware store routinely finds himself in the middle of). If that seems like a worthwhile goal, read on.

Part I

Foundation Concepts

| CHAPTER 1 |

"Before We Begin . . ."

It is wise to keep in mind that neither success nor failure is ever final.

—ROGER BABSON

- ◆ What's a good way to take the early initiative in conversations with prospects and customers?
- ◆ How can you gather important information very early on in the relationship?
- ◆ What are the foundations of an effective selling strategy?
- ◆ Are we putting the principles of effective selling into practice each and every selling day?

WHEN I AM TRAINING SALESPEOPLE during our company's seminars, I tell the story of a young salesperson who came to meet with me to try to sell me advertising space in the yellow pages. I asked him to wait in the lobby while I completed a few tasks in my office. But before he sat down in the lobby, I asked him, "Before we begin, what's the first question you plan to ask me when we get together?"

By making this query, I was, of course, *beginning* the meeting.

But he nodded enthusiastically and said, "Before we get started, I guess it does makes sense for me to think a little bit about the first question. Usually, what I ask is, are you happy with your advertising?"

"And," I asked him, "what do people usually say when you ask them that?"

"Well," he said, "usually they tell me that they're happy with their advertising."

"And what happens then?"

"Well, at that point, I usually ask if they have any questions, and if they don't, I move on to my next meeting. After all, I've qualified them."

I will not bother sharing with you the rest of our discussion, except to say that I did not end up buying yellow pages advertising from that salesperson. But notice how much information about his sales process I was able to elicit "before we began" the meeting!

I think that is the way a lot of good sales strategy works. You find a way to get some kind of meaningful information out on the table "before you begin"—and that is the way I want to start this book. There is a lot to look at, but before we even begin, I want to share with you some important information . . . information that might just help you to take an approach to selling that is a little bit more constructive than the approach that yellow pages representative took during his meeting with me.

So—before we begin—here are twelve simple, career-changing pieces of advice I have been sharing for years with salespeople.

The list, which is the culmination of over a quarter of a century of experience, may be brief, but I've noticed that those who follow all twelve rules always seem to outearn those who don't.

1. Always respond to customer queries within forty-eight hours.
2. Schedule sales appointments for early (8 A.M.) or late (4 P.M.).
3. Follow through immediately on thank-you letters, letters of agreement, and internal paperwork.
4. Set two new appointments every day.
5. Strategize with your sales manager on a regular basis.
6. Don't kid yourself.
7. Create a sense of urgency in all your communications.
8. Be honest.
9. Know ten client success stories.
10. Decide on your opening question for the meeting.
11. Decide on the Next Step you want and ask for it directly.
12. Always try to get the other person to *do* something.

Here's my challenge to you: Put these principles of effective selling into practice each and every selling day.

| CHAPTER 2 |

What Is Upselling?

God gave us two ends. One to sit on and one to think with.
Success depends on which one you use; heads, you win—tails,
you lose.

—Anonymous

♦ How can we define the process of upselling?
♦ What are some challenges related to upselling?
♦ How is it different from the "static" sales model some sales-people are familiar with?
♦ What are the economic reasons for improving an organization's upselling strategies?
♦ What is the genesis of the ideas covered in this book?

Upselling is what happens when you take the initiative to ask someone who already has purchased something you offer to purchase more of it—or more of something else.

This can happen in a variety of ways and over a variety of different time spans.

- *Upselling* happens when a TV infomercial concludes with an appeal to call a toll-free number . . . and the customer, after placing the order, responds positively to an appeal to purchase a different product, too
- *Upselling* happens when an order is shipped from a manufac-turing plant, and the manufacturer includes, with the invoice, a flyer about an additional product or service that thanks the

customer for his or her business . . . and alerts him or her to a special offering this month.

- *Upselling* also takes place when there is a decision to expand a business relationship with you or your company over the long term. So, for instance, in my company, where we sell sales training, upselling takes place after we have delivered the initial program, and it allows us to deliver more training in the weeks and months that follow.

Upselling is a never-ending process. This is what makes it a challenge for some people. They like to think of the sales process as something that is static, something that begins at point A and ends at point D, or E, or F. While there is certainly a lot to learn by evaluating the sales process in this linear way, it is just as true that upselling is an essential component of any successful sales career, team, or indeed of any successful organization.

Why Should You Try Upselling?

It is a well-known sales and business maxim that it costs significantly less to generate new business from an existing customer than it does to generate a new customer from scratch. In this book, you will be looking at a number of ways to create business with existing customers, and you will learn a variety of strategies for kick-starting this phenomenon of expanding the orders you receive from your customers, whether in the short or the long term.

So, if your job is to sell over the phone and you want to be able to expand the average size of your order during a single-call close—that is, a conversation that ends with the customer's decision to buy not only your primary product, but something else, too—you will find advice on doing that here.

If your goal is to be able to reach out to existing customers and give them good reasons to buy more of what you sell, you will find that here as well.

The ideas you will encounter in this book are basic—"simple." But for all their simplicity, they are rarely carried out by salespeople in the real world. The genesis of the ideas covered in this book is worth noting. We train other people with these principles because we tested them ourselves, and we use them ourselves! What you will read here is the result of twenty-five years of trial and error. Give it an honest try.

Take advantage of the system that follows. It works! Read it. Understand it. And then implement it. Hold yourself to the standard that a good idea, even one that sounds "simple," is worse than useless if left untried.

| CHAPTER 3 |

Upselling Is a Conversation

The trouble with her is that she lacks the power of conversation but not the power of speech.
—GEORGE BERNARD SHAW

♦ What is the foundation of upselling?
♦ How does the salesperson's curiosity affect the upselling process?
♦ What are "do-based" questions?
♦ Why shouldn't we focus on need, pain, or problems in our discussions with customers?

WHETHER WE REALIZE IT OR NOT, upselling is based on relationships. And the only real relationships we can count on are those that arise out of intelligent conversations between two people. Conversations are the foundation of upselling.

I wish I could give you some magic wand that you could wave over your prospects that would instantly allow them to see the benefits of buying more of your product, but no such magic wand exists. In the end, we will upsell, or fail to upsell, based on the quality of our conversations with our prospects and customers. If we display genuine curiosity and ask appropriate do-based questions, we will sell more of our products and services to our customers. If we don't, we won't.

You may well ask, What are do-based questions?

Do-based questions are questions that focus, not on what we think the other person *needs*, or what we think his or her *problem* is, or what we think the potential *pain* is, but on what the other person is actually *doing*. If we focus only on what we consider the need, the pain, or the problem, then we won't get the whole picture of what's happening in the other person's world. We may get part of that picture, and we may close an initial sale, but to build a relationship for the future, we have to be willing to ask questions about what the other person *does*. For instance:

- "Hey, we've talked about your current salespeople—but how are you handling your training for your new hires right now?"
- "How long have you been trying to sell your motorcycle? What have you been doing to sell it so far?"
- "How did you handle this kind of staffing problem the last time around?"

All of these are do-based questions. And all of them are substantial improvements over silly questions like, "What would you change about your current so-and-so?" or "What don't you like about your present situation?"

Effective upselling is an extended conversation that allows you to find out what the other person is doing and plans to do, review key objectives, and make those objectives your own.

If you never learn or even bother to ask about what this person is doing or what this person's objectives are on the job or in other realms of his life, then you will not be in much of a position to expand the relationship with your customers.

CHAPTER 4

Selling by Not Selling

Have no fear of perfection—you'll never reach it.
—SALVADOR DALI

- ♦ Why does the saying "less is more" apply particularly to upselling?
- ♦ How can we use non-sales-related discussions to move the upselling process forward?
- ♦ What's a good way to reestablish contact with a customer who's fallen off our "radar screen"?
- ♦ How can we use the "power" of paying attention to the customer to our advantage?

WHEN IT COMES TO MOVING TOWARD that elusive goal—perfection in upselling—we sometimes find that less is more.

Each and every interaction with a customer we hope to sell more to—especially those interactions that are *not* directly sales oriented—is, in fact, a selling opportunity. How's that for a paradox? These nonselling discussions are chances to deepen the relationship, expand our knowledge base about what is going on in an organization and in the other person's life, and pass along relevant suggestions that parallel our own experience and ability to add value.

The bottom line: You sell when you don't sell.

Let's say, for the sake of argument, that I am attempting to review the yearly training plan with a major account of my company. This contact is someone who has done a lot of business with our firm and someone who has in the past had no problem sitting down with me to review what his training plans are for the coming year. Let's say we have been working together for three or four years. Now, all of a sudden, the person vanishes off the radar screen. I want to upsell to this person—that is, sell even more training to him—but my e-mails have gone unreturned, my voice mail messages have vanished into the ether, and my attempts to reach out to other people in the organization have gone nowhere. What can I do?

The best answer, in my view, is to give the person a reason to take my call that does not have to do with selling. In other words, I might send the person a book or article (that is, physically send an actual book, not e-mail an excerpt or chapter) with a personalized note. At that point, I would allow three or four days for the mail to deliver the book. I can then call and leave a message *asking what the person thought of the book or article.*

I am giving the person an easy way to respond and giving him a conflict-free context for future conversation. If there's something there, I'll probably hear back from the person—or be able to reach him more easily the next time around.

I'll do anything to avoid the call that sounds like this: "Hi John, haven't heard from you in a while—just wondering whether you had the chance to look at my proposal."

Far better to call a current customer *to add value to his or her day—and let the "selling" emerge of its own momentum during the conversation through "do-based" questioning!*

Here's what I say at the end of the conversation about the book or article I sent along: "Just out of curiosity, John—can we get together for lunch next Tuesday at 2:00? I have an idea I want to bounce off you."

Some years ago, Robert Morse starred on Broadway in a one-man show entitled *Tru.* In that show, he offered a dead-on performance of the author Truman Capote. Capote was, as you may know, a brilliant, ultimately self-destructive literary genius. One of the more remarkable sections of the play came when Morris, as Capote, offered his advice on how to get anyone—repeat, anyone—to fall in love with you.

The advice, according to Capote, was actually very simple. Simply pay attention to the other person as though he or she were the only person on earth. Do that consistently, day in and day out, and regardless of the other obstacles in the relationship, you will find yourself united with this person.

It's a fascinating piece of advice, advice that is relevant to the business world as well as the world of personal relationships. Ultimately, the guiding principle for good sales conversations, or upselling, and for all aspects of person-to-person selling is simply to pay a heck of a lot of attention to the other person. Not "sales" attention. Real attention.

Be absolutely certain that, when you are in a meeting with your contact, interacting with him or her on the phone, or sending an e-mail, you are sending the message that this person really is more important than anything or anyone else on earth. Forget about selling. Just focus on what the other person is doing with incredible focus and attention.

If you can follow through on that type of commitment, genuine interest, and unapologetic attention, you will attract interest, you will build a relationship, and you will be able to sell more to your current customers.

| CHAPTER 5 |

"It Makes Sense!"

To guarantee success, act as if it were impossible to fail.
—DOROTHEA BRANDE

♦ What does the initial buying process look like?
♦ Why do people buy products and services—what motivates them?
♦ What's the best "closing" strategy?
♦ What's the difference between selling and order taking?
♦ What role does information gathering play in our sales process?
♦ What role do commonality and rapport play in our sales process?

IN ORDER TO UNDERSTAND how people can buy more from us, we have to understand how they decide to buy from us in the first place.

To get an idea of how that process works, I want to ask you to think about the last purchase that you made that involved more than $100. (The same principles are at work in just about any purchase, but they are a little easier to see and remember if we focus in on purchases that require more than $100.)

Have you got that recent purchase in mind? Great. Now, let me ask you something. Why did you decide to make the purchase that you did?

Whatever your answer is, I am willing to bet that the underlying reason for your decision to make the purchase that you did was actually very simple: It made sense for you to do so.

There are any number of variations on this "makes sense" reasoning. It made sense for you to purchase a car for your family *because* you needed to be able to get the kids back and forth from home to camp and from camp to band practice, and so on. It made sense for you to buy the particular car that you did *because* the car you looked at was rated highly for safety, was available at a good price, had good recommendations from your relatives, and so forth. Whatever the actual reasons were, I think if you look closely at them you will find that they really do emerge as footnotes or elaborations on the statement "It made sense for me." If you buy a piece of exercise equipment, you do so because it makes sense for you based on your goals in terms of personal fitness. If you buy an insurance policy, you do so because it makes sense for you in terms of the protection you want to give to your family. That is how purchasing works. We only do what makes sense to us. And conversely, if it does not make sense to us, we are not going to do it. There is no way anyone will ever purchase anything based on the conviction that the purchase really does not make any sense.

So, let's think of the final step in the sales process as this decision that something makes sense. That is from the buyer's point of view. From the seller's point of view, we think of this as a "close"—although, in fact, there is very little that is actually closing and, given the focus of this book, it might be better to think of it as an "open."

We are not really closing up the relationship as much as we are opening it to the whole universe of possible future decisions to buy. The term *closing* is so prevalent in the sales profession that it probably makes sense for us to use it here, if only for clarity's sake.

And by the way, our formal "closing technique" is rooted in this "makes sense" principle. Here's what we train people to say when they want to close a deal, whether it's the first piece of business they get from a contact or the hundredth piece of business:

"Makes sense to me—what do you think?"

That's our whole closing strategy!

Now, from the salesperson's point of view, it is nice when someone decides *on their own* that it make sense to purchase something from us. But it does not happen often enough for us to be able to count on that revenue. So we have to go out and make something happen. We have to get in front of people and help move the process forward to the degree that we are capable of doing so. Otherwise we are basically taking orders.

There is nothing wrong with taking orders, but in terms of one's responsibilities as a professional salesperson, simply waiting for the phone to ring and doing nothing but taking orders really does not fit the bill.

So how do we get the person to decide that it makes sense to buy what we offer?

This is a simple question, and it brings us to the step immediately before the closing step, which is what I call the *presentation or proposal step*. Actually, even though this phase involves, from our point of view, a presentation or proposal, from the buyer's point of view, it is nothing more or less than the *reason* that it really does make sense to buy from us. So, to go back to the example of the car that we purchased to get our kids from point A to point B, the reasons for my decision to purchase a car could be that I want it to cost less than $25,000, that I want it to have a high safety rating, and that I want to get good gas mileage. Those might be my three "hot button" reasons for purchasing an automobile. The problem for the seller is, of course, that he will have no idea what my reason for purchasing a car might be. It is entirely possible that I have not even articulated the reasons effectively myself. But I will respond positively or negatively to certain reasons that are proposed to me.

Consider this question: How many *possible* reasons to buy a car could there be? Actually, there are quite a few, but most of them will not actually match up with my own personal reasons for buying one. In other words, if the salesperson at the automobile showroom insists on talking to me about the fact that the car can go 120 miles an hour, that is not going to be a motivator for me. If he tells me that the car is going to enhance my sex appeal as I am cruising up and down the boulevard, that is not going to be a big motivator for me, either, as the main reason I am trying to purchase the automobile is to get my kids from point A to point B. You will notice that there are many, many *potential* reasons that I could buy a car, but only a very narrow set of actual reasons that I *would* purchase a car.

The question that arises is, How does somebody who is trying to sell a car to me determine which are the right reasons and which are the ones to bother with?

This very important issue brings us to the steps that precede the presentation or reason phase of the sale. It is with this issue that we come face-to-face with the most important part of the selling process—namely, the *information-gathering step*. Take a look at this graphic:

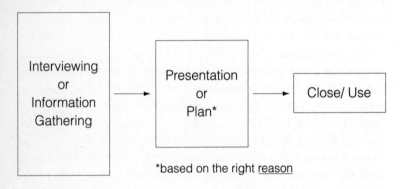

*based on the right <u>reason</u>

You will notice that the information-gathering piece is significantly larger than the presentation or closing in our ideal sales model. This is because I strongly recommend that approximately 75 percent of the salesperson's time and effort be invested in information gathering and presentation preparation. In other words, three-quarters of the work has to come before we make any formal recommendation. And it is in this information-gathering phase that we determine which motivators precisely are likely to be the ones that will resonate with our prospective customer. So during this phase, we would expect the salesperson in the showroom to find out a little bit more about me and my family, what made me decide to walk into the showroom that day, how many kids I am responsible for shuttling around, and so forth. If he or she manages this portion of the sales process intelligently—and that might well mean not trying to close the sale in the first visit, but reaching out to me by phone after I have spent an initial visit in the showroom—the interesting thing is that the salesperson will not only develop the appropriate information about my auto buying requirements, but he will also establish a certain amount of rapport with me as a person. He will get to know how I make decisions, what my preconceptions about automobiles are, what my speaking style is, and so forth.

Now, from a salesperson's point of view, we might like to think that these three steps are all that is involved in selling effectively. But the hard facts of human nature suggest otherwise. If I walk into the showroom and the car salesman instantly pounces on me and starts peppering me with questions about my family, my past history of purchasing automobiles, my reasons for walking into the showroom, and so forth, he is not going to close many sales. In fact, there is a precursor to all three of the steps that we have outlined here, and it is a very important one that we call the opening or greeting phase.

This is also known sometimes as the *qualifying phase.* It is an initial portion of the relationship where the salesperson establishes some kind of commonality or rapport with the person he or she has identified as a prospect. It can also be the part of the relationship where the salesperson makes a quick assessment as to whether or not this is a realistic prospect or a prospect at all. Both of these things basically happen at the same time, and if you put that phase of the relationship on the far left-hand corner of the model, you can see the entire process, at least for the initial purchase:

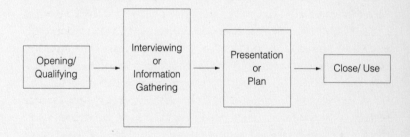

In the initial phase, on the far left of the description, you will find the opening of the relationship. And as I say, commonality is a big part of what happens. You studied such-and-such in school—what a coincidence, so did I! You made a certain career choice recently—and that's genuinely interesting to me because I made a very similar choice a few years back.

So, in the initial discussion with my prospect, I am going to find elements that he or she has in common with me.

After a while, you learn to build up commonality with just about anyone. Honestly, I don't care who you put in front of me, I can find something I have in common with that person. If you bring me a tribesman from Nigeria and sit him down across from my desk in midtown Manhattan, I can find something that I have in common with that individual. We might, for instance, have a shared interest in making sure that the environment is protected and that local agriculture be allowed to flourish in harmony with it. The point is that a good salesperson finds reasons to discuss things that he or she has in common with other people. And perhaps just as important, a good salesperson finds a way to discuss these things *in a communication style that matches that of the prospect.*

So if the other person speaks quickly, I am going to try to match that person's tone and rate of speed. If the other person is slower and more sober and reflective, I am going to try to find a way to match that as well.

CHAPTER 6

Verification

If only God would give me some clear sign that I'm on the right track! Like making a large deposit in my name at a Swiss bank.

—Woody Allen

- ◆ What is the verification substep?
- ◆ How does it fit into the sales process?
- ◆ Why is it so important?
- ◆ How is it related to the information-gathering process?
- ◆ How can you confirm that you're thinking along the same lines as the customer about what should happen next?

There is one additional substep that we need to add to this process for purchasing something, and it is what is known as the *verification substep*.

Verifying is an important element of the sales process because our information tends to improve in quality as the length of the relationship with a person increases. What this means is that the information I share with the automobile sales representative in the first five minutes of my conversation with him is not necessarily going to be as meaningful or as accurate as the information I share with him a week and a half later during our third conversation—or even half an hour later during the *same* conversation.

As we get to know people better and as we open up to them more fully, we fill in the blanks, offer additional facts, and even correct misperceptions that we may have, for various reasons, left in our initial conversations with the person. The bottom line is that we trust people with whom we have had an extended series of conversations more than we trust people whom we have just met. As a result, not every single solitary piece of information that a salesperson writes down in his or her notebook is going to be technically accurate by the time the interview phase is complete. In fact, the interview can look complete when, in fact, it is not complete. And that is where the verification substep comes in.

I strongly recommend some kind of "replaying" of basic information *before* you make any attempt to close the sale or make formal recommendations. This verification can take any number of forms, but it is important.

And here is where upselling enters the equation. Consider the example of the automobile dealership. If the product is right, and the quality is high, and if the reasons for suggesting the purchase really do match up with what I am actually looking to make happen in my life in terms of transport for my family, then that auto dealership has the right to hope and expect that I will come back to them for the next car. And, in fact, this is exactly how the best dealerships and the best automakers function. They build up high degrees of trust and communication with their prospects, they deliver on the promises that they make to their sales prospects, and they assure that their customers' satisfaction with their products is high both in terms of initial product quality and also in service and repair. So that after four or five years or however long it takes me to decide I need a new car, it would be much easier for me to return to that same dealership and that same manufacturer, and move up the ladder to the next model of car that seems appropriate for me.

So, you can see that the sales process itself does not operate in a vacuum, but is, in fact, geared toward repeat purchases if you do it correctly.

In any upselling conversation, whether it is for a multimillion-dollar piece of construction equipment or a $2.99 monthly commitment to a magazine, there is a powerful sentence you can use to get a clear sense of precisely where your customer stands in relation to your offer: "Here's what I'm getting so far . . ."

Verification

This statement is one that has to follow some kind of intelligent questioning that features genuine curiosity of what is happening in the other person's world. Once you have done that, try to determine precisely where you stand by replaying key information *and* how you interpret it, by saying, "Here's what I'm getting so far . . ." You can then say, "Based on what you're telling me, this is what I'm thinking of recommending," and then ask, "Are we thinking along the same lines?"

CHAPTER 7

Remember Why People Buy!

No matter what anybody tells you, words and ideas can change the world.
—ROBIN WILLIAMS, IN *DEAD POETS SOCIETY*

♦ Why is the plan we put together for the customer so important?
♦ How much time should we spend in the information-gathering phase?
♦ What makes a successful presentation possible?
♦ What must precede the interviewing or information-gathering step?
♦ What does the process look like when you put all the steps together?

I WANT TO EMPHASIZE THAT THE DECISION to buy from us in the first place does not happen out of thin air. It happens because the person decides to buy into our plan and use what we have to offer. Why would somebody do that? The answer is simple. They only choose to use what we sell if it makes sense to them to do so. Whether they call us up and ask us to come in and solve a problem, or we call them up and eventually make a presentation that they sign off on, the only reason the person ultimately decides to buy from us is that it really makes sense for them to do so—from their point of view. So what causes that decision to happen?

The answer in many cases is the proposal or plan or reason that we have given them for deciding to buy. If that reason is strong enough and compelling enough, and if we have elucidated it correctly, we are going to get the sale. If the reason that we give helps the person to *do* what he or she is already doing, we are going to get the sale.

But how do we get that reason or plan? Well, that goes to the step before the presentation. That is, the information-gathering stage. Notice that it is impossible to deliver a good presentation, a presentation that wins a sale, if we do not have the information we need. In my training sessions, I emphasize the important point that one must, realistically, expect to spend 75 percent of the sales process in the information-gathering phase—notice how big that phase is in the model I have given you.

Nevertheless, it is a fact of life that we cannot simply barge into the process office and begin asking questions. We must qualify or open the sale. That means developing a little bit of rapport, usually by means of some kind of small talk.

Notice that all four of these processes are interrelated and that each one must unfold out of the previous step. This is the microcosm of the sale. This is a map of what happens when we do not know someone and we turn them into a customer.

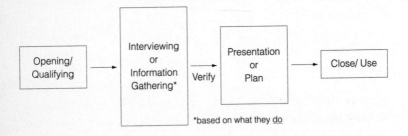

CHAPTER 8

Offer, Timetable, Price

You only have to do a very few things right in your life so long as you don't do too many things wrong.
—WARREN BUFFETT

♦ What are the critical topics of discussion that are likely to come up during any selling or upselling process?
♦ What should we do if we find ourselves hitting an obstacle in one of these areas?
♦ How can we keep the process moving forward?
♦ What's the best way to keep minor obstacles from becoming major ones?

AT ANY GIVEN MOMENT during the upselling initiative you may be presenting, there are three items that may be under discussion. They are:

1. *The offer itself.* This means the specifics of the equipment, service, or program that you want the customer to consider as an additional purchase.
2. *The timetable.* This is the point in time at which you would deliver or implement your additional sale.
3. *The terms.* This is how your customer would end up paying for the additional purchase.

There is an interesting rule of thumb in upselling that you may want to consider once you have identified these three elements of your sale. It is really amazingly simple, and it is one of those ideas that lead people to wonder why they did not think of it, once they encounter it for the first time. Basically, it is this: If you are having trouble dealing with one of these three elements, simply change gears and try to focus on one of the other two.

In other words, do not let the fact that the person has grave doubts about your payment schedule keep you from discussing the specifics of the offer or the possible timetable. Get as much buy-in as you can on those other two items, and emphasize the points that are most in line with what this person is already doing. Rather than hammering on whether or not you can get a special deal on the payment terms, step back and find a way to focus on your common interests: the benefits that the person will receive from your offer and the timetable that makes the most sense for him or her to receive those benefits.

Far too many salespeople lose the opportunity to add revenue to their sale by focusing on the "letter of the law" with regard to one of these three key points. They will say things like "I can't change the specifications" or "I can't change the timing" or "I can't change the pricing." Whether or not that is true—and in most cases it turns out not to be true—you really do not gain any rapport or additional information by harping on such points. Focus on what is working in one of the other two areas, and move on to the minor detail of working out the issues in that third category.

CHAPTER 9

Essential Upselling Principles

Success is a journey, not a destination.
—BEN SWEETLAND

♦ What are the essential principles of upselling?
♦ What role does time play in your upselling efforts?
♦ What are the hallmarks of the effective interviewer?

TO BE A SUCCESSFUL UPSELLER:

1. You must convey excitement about what you do.
2. You must know when to be quiet.
3. You must Keep It Simple, Stupid (KISS).
4. You must have an open mind at each step of the sales process. (No preconceptions!)
5. You must have a defensive sales strategy and anticipate what could go wrong. (Think one step ahead.)
6. You must temper zeal with pragmatism.
7. You must never minimize the role of the administrative staff at the target company, particularly executive assistants.
8. You must avoid keeping the wrong prospect in play for too long. In other words, you must know your own time cycle, and you must learn when to recognize that you are spending too much time, energy, and attention on an opportunity that is not moving forward during that average selling cycle. There really is an average period of time that it takes a current customer to move from the "initial discussions" phase to a decision to do more work with you. Your job is to find out

what that average period of time is—and honor it. If you consistently invest significantly *longer* periods of time than that in your upselling, there's a problem, and you need to take a close look at your time choices.

9. You must learn to develop a realistic sense of what the target company wants to do with you. (Don't overvalue!)
10. You must maintain control of the meeting and the sales process as a whole.
11. You must monitor how much time you spend developing outlines and proposals.
12. You must learn to charge what you're worth. (Don't undervalue yourself; don't sell yourself short when determining the value you bring to the organization.)
13. You must remember that each relationship you build will stay with you over the long term.
14. You must think positively—and think big!
15. You must be an effective interviewer.

That last item is particularly near and dear to my heart. Bear in mind that a good interviewer is:

- Genuinely curious
- Interested in what the other person does
- Interested in how the company makes a profit
- Interested in how the company holds off competitive challenges
- Not product focused and not eager to move into what he or she wants to say
- Willing to ask "how" and "why" questions
- Curious about what makes this person unique
- Willing to ask questions to which he or she does not always have the answer

Here's another important principle to remember about interviewing: *Don't ask, don't sell.* What do I mean by that? If you do not ask any questions, you cannot expect to gather any meaningful information. And if you do not gather any meaningful information, you cannot expect to expand the relationship.

| CHAPTER 10 |

Key Communication Principles

If it's the Psychic Network,
why do they need a phone number?
—ROBIN WILLIAMS

♦ How should you prepare for the information-gathering phase?
♦ What does "People respond in kind" mean?
♦ What does "We create the flow" mean?
♦ How can we anticipate responses?
♦ How can we put the fact that people communicate through stories to work for our upselling process?
♦ What do stories tell you about the culture of the organization you're selling to?

THERE ARE THREE fundamental communication principles that can support your effort to sell more to your customer.

Principle #1: *People Respond in Kind; We Create the Flow*

As we have seen, upselling is a conversation, and effective upsellers must learn to master that conversation. An essential first element of mastering the art of the conversation, especially the upselling conversation, lies in understanding this first principle.

When Katie Couric secures an interview with an extremely important figure—the president of the United States, say—do you think she simply sits down and improvises her way through the conversation without any preparation at all? Does she allow herself the luxury of a long game of tennis the day before the interview, contenting herself with the knowledge that the president will certainly think of something interesting to say?

My guess is that Katie has a set of very interesting questions all ready, a list that she has reviewed many times, before she steps into her interview with the president. In fact, I would even go further and propose that Katie very likely allows herself a couple of different roadways for each question, depending on the response that she gets from the president! (More on this idea in a moment.)

My point here is that there is no point in winging it in your discussions with customers. They are every bit as important to you as the discussion with the president of the United States is to Katie Couric—if not more so. So, instead of wondering what is going to happen during the conversation, it makes much more sense to understand the vital role your choice of a question will play in setting the dynamic and the flow of the conversation. The reason your question is so important is that people will respond to the topics that you raise, just as the president will, of necessity, say something about the topic Katie Couric raises during her interview with him. Mind you, the president may not answer with precisely the same level of specificity that Katie might like, but the topic she raises will, without fail, influence the direction in which the conversation goes. If you want the conversation to proceed along a path that is beneficial to you, you will first need to identify what that path is, and then follow through by posing a series of questions that will point the conversation in that direction.

For example, when I am meeting with a representative of a company whom I wish to do more business with, my initial question is absolutely clear to me. Depending on the client, I might ask what the person has decided about expanding into a certain market; I might ask how the competition is doing in a new product release; or I might ask, "Where do you see us being able to add value in your South American operations?"

After the handshake and the pleasantry phase, I always have some specific question that I will use to determine the direction of the conversation. And I know I will be able to point the conversation in that direction because people will respond in kind to what I ask. After all, if I ask you, "How are you feeling today?" you are not going to respond by talking about peach ice cream.

Principle #2: *Some Responses Can Be Anticipated*

I said a little earlier that, when Katie Couric prepares for her interview with the president of the United States, she thinks about where her questions will go. This is another way of saying that she knows ahead of time that any president or presidential candidate—or, indeed, any politician worth his or her salt—will probably not give a direct answer to the question that she asks. For instance, if she were to ask a sitting president the question that his or her challenger during an election year would most want answered, the likely outcome would *not* be a direct response to the points in the question. Instead, she would have to expect a certain amount of rhetorical dancing, bobbing, and weaving. But here is the point: If she is really doing her job, *she will know that ahead of time* and prepare a follow-up question or response of her own in order to put the president's response into some kind of context for the interview.

What Katie Couric and any other good interviewer knows is that a discussion with a public figure, a colleague, or an upselling prospect should not simply be a series of memorized questions. You cannot walk in the door and assume that the same questions that you have identified for your interview are going to be the best structure for that interview. You cannot simply rattle off all of those questions in sequence. Instead, you have to be ready for responses. And even one step further than that, you have to know what you will say back when you hear those responses.

Now, as a salesperson, your job is considerably easier than that of a journalist. For one thing, you are not out to "get" your interview partner, and you are certainly not out to prove him or her inconsistent in the same way that a good reporter may try to highlight any inconsistencies in a discussion with a politician. However, the central dynamic of knowing that a response will be coming, and being able to prepare for it, is exactly the same. In fact, this dynamic is a good deal more pronounced in the sales world, because the same kinds of responses come up again and again for people who have been selling for more than a few weeks. We have heard it all. We know the budget is too tight, we know that people have no time, we know that there are certain technical constraints that may prevent certain constituencies from deciding that it is a great idea to work with us . . . we know the drill. I am even willing to bet that if you took the time right now, you could identify ten objections—or, to use a more accurate term, initial negative responses—that you hear over and over again from your own prospects and customers. In particular, I will bet you could identify the types of questions, issues, and challenges that come up with your customers during your discussions about the best ways to extend your relationship with them.

If your sale is at all like mine, you encounter the same issues from customer A, in a slightly different form, or even in an identical form, as you do from customers B, C, D, and E. Here is the point: We can anticipate these responses. We can predict. We can predict and prepare for the responses we hear every day. And we can know exactly the right story or anecdote from our own experience or that of someone else on our sales team that will help us to address whatever issue has arisen.

For instance, suppose I am talking to someone who is eager to get more training from my company after having had a good initial program. It is common for us to hear that "the financing does not work." My contact will say, "Steve, we want to do the program, but our training budget is exhausted for the next two months, and we really can't make any commitment until June."

Now the first time I heard this, I could perhaps be excused for not having any intelligent response or story to share about it. But having been in this business for twenty-five years, I take some pride in being able to say, whenever I hear this response, that we have done a lot of work with customers who faced exactly this situation. And what we have done in the past, in order to address the problem, is simply schedule the date, allocate our own training time, get the company's people trained in the new processes they need, and bill against the next quarter. That is much better from my point of view, because I would rather get the business than not. And it is much better from the customer's point of view than leaving a team that has just been trained in one program without any further training for two or three months until the next program materializes.

That is an example from my industry, and I am sure you can come up with examples from your own without too much difficulty. The one point you do have to bear in mind, however, is that despite how similar some of the objections and responses and issues we hear may sound, they really are coming from a unique person and a unique organization. So you will want to be very careful not to assume that the dimensions of the problem are *precisely* the same as those of the last person you heard this issue from. Instead, you will need to express your understanding of what the person has said, replay what you have heard, and then share an interesting anecdote from your own history. You're going to express your opinion that you might be able to take a similar approach here, and then ask the person whether or not you are both thinking along the same lines.

Principle #3: *People Communicate Through Stories*

You will notice, in the way I explained communication principle #2, that I emphasized the importance of my sharing a story from my own company's history in response to an issue that had come up from the customer. That is obviously a great way to go, but it is not as powerful as getting the *other person* to share one of his or her stories.

People love to tell stories, and they often base their own decisions about whether to keep buying from us not only on the stories that we share with them, but also on the stories that they decide to share with us.

In fact, I think it is probably fair to say that one tangible piece of evidence of success in the information-gathering process is the ability to point to a story that the customer has shared with you. By asking questions like "How did you handle that?" or "What made you decide to work for the company?" or "What kind of place is this to work?" we are trying to get factual information, but we are also trying to get the customer to open up to us and share a story that is uniquely informative about his or her career or the organization's development.

You can make an argument that stories are what form corporate culture. In other words, if you were an employee at the company you are trying to sell more of your products and services to, you would know certain critical stories about the company's viewpoint and history. Some stories are all about the company's internal philosophy: how the founder drove through thirty-five snowy miles of rough terrain to deliver a shipment on time, for instance. Some stories will give you all the information you need about the internal politics that you face in dealing with a customer's internal communications challenges. For instance, you might hear a story about how difficult the legal team is to keep satisfied and how important they are in the hierarchy since the company faced an unexpected series of product liability lawsuits. Whatever the story is, there is only one thing you can be certain of: If you have not heard a story from your prospect about what his or her world looks like, you have not gotten all the important information yet. Consider it your goal to share your own relevant success stories with each and every upselling contact in your own world, and to ask the intelligent questions and encourage the lengthy responses that will lead you toward the stories that mark the boundaries of the world of the person to whom you are trying to sell.

Part II

On the Phone

CHAPTER 11

Why Telesales Is So Tough

Flaming enthusiasm, backed by horse sense and persistence,
is the quality that most frequently makes for success.
—DALE CARNEGIE

♦ What special challenges do telesales professionals face?
♦ What kind of preparation is necessary for success as a telesales professional?
♦ Why are praise and recognition harder to come by in this line of work?
♦ What role do managers sometimes play in making the telesales professional's work more challenging?
♦ How does all this affect the job of upselling?

LET'S TALK A LITTLE BIT about what upselling looks like in the telesales environment. I like to focus special attention and energy on the challenge of the telemarketers and training programs, because I honestly believe that telesales is one of the most difficult kinds of selling.

Why do I say that telesales is one of the most difficult selling jobs? There are a number of reasons. For one thing, you cannot see the person you are selling to. We know for a fact that the majority of human communication occurs through nonverbal signals, and yet the telesales professional must perform his or her job without any indication of the other person's facial expression, posture, gaze, or even whether the person is doing something else entirely unrelated while we are speaking with them! We have only the person's tone of voice to go on, and that really does leave us at a major disadvantage.

Another reason that people working in telesales have it so very difficult is that they usually have to be better prepared than a field salesperson does. I say that because the telesales environment is usually highly compressed. When a field salesperson closes the sale, it is usually as a result of two or three (or four or five or six) weeks' worth of work, and sometimes much more work than that. But while the payoff may—or may not—be higher, the telesales professional must close his or her sale typically in one or two or three telephone conversations. Sometimes the "sales cycle" is a single telephone call.

Another reason telesales is among the most difficult ways to sell for a living is that recognition and praise are a little harder to come by. This is another way of saying that the profession is fraught with stereotypes, and the task of selling for a living over the telephone often does not come with the same praise and recognition from friends, relatives, and even colleagues within the organization as the job of selling face-to-face does. I know a good many telesales professionals who sell highly specialized and very expensive technical solutions and who make a great deal of money doing so. What I find particularly interesting is that they always find ways to change the title of what they do for a living! They do not want to be confused with the "average" telesales representative. This is a stigma that makes the job more difficult. I will not even go into the social standing of those in this type of selling, and the media stereotypes that are perpetuated about them.

Probably one of the clearest indications telesales is a very difficult kind of selling is that people who sell in this environment hear more frequent—and harsher—*no* answers than just about anybody else who sells. If you set an appointment to meet with someone a week from now, and you walked in the door to talk to that person, it is very unlikely that he will look you in the face, ask you what the heck you are doing in his office, and order you out brusquely. But it is a very common occurrence, indeed an occupational hazard, for a telesales professional to be greeted with rudeness, obscenity, and hang-ups. In fact, for most people who sell over the phone, it is a very unusual day indeed when they do not encounter this demoralizing kind of response. As in any profession, of course, that there are good telesales professionals and less skilled telesales professionals. Unfortunately, even those who do everything "right" and want to approach their jobs professionally are held accountable, within the first fifteen seconds of the conversation, for the perceived sins and shortcomings of all the others who have fumbled the assignment with that prospect over the past month or so.

Yet another reason that telesales is one of the most difficult kinds of selling is that telesales representatives are more closely observed by their managers. Whereas a successful field representative earns a certain measure of autonomy and is sometimes a beneficiary of the mindset that says "As long as you hit quota, I don't care how you spend your day," there are very few telesales representatives for whom this is the coaching model. (Whether or not this hands-off approach is a workable coaching model, of course, is another subject.) The fact remains that, whereas field representatives do not have the prospect of their sales visits being recorded and reviewed, or the number of discussions that they initiate evaluated from a computer bank, telesales professionals do. Whether this is a good thing or a bad thing is not at issue here. I am simply pointing out that this can be an added stress in the position and that many telesales representatives are monitored by inept managers.

One special set of challenges makes telesales difficult for certain categories of telesales professionals, in particular those involved in the inbound sales process. Whereas outbound telesales people make calls to people on a more or less restricted basis, there is a time management challenge that is unique to people whose job is exclusively related to inbound selling, namely, that their daily workflow experience hits peaks and valleys. In other words, there are periods of intense activity and periods of dormant activity, when the phone is not ringing, and the question of how to manage and balance these cycles is sometimes poorly addressed by managers.

Last but not least, among the reasons contributing to the fact that telesales is a difficult way to make a living, and a difficult environment in which to upsell, is the fact that, as a general rule, compensation schemes tend to be lower—indeed, significantly lower—for the telesales professionals than for other people who sell for a living. This adds to the stress of the job and makes burnout and high turnover rates more likely.

All of these stresses affect the job of upselling in a predictable way. They make it much more difficult.

| CHAPTER 12 |

By the Numbers

Success is the ability to go from failure to failure without losing your enthusiasm.

—Sir Winston Churchill

- ♦ Why is monitoring numbers and activity important?
- ♦ How do activity numbers relate to one another as ratios?
- ♦ What do inbound activity numbers look like?
- ♦ What do outbound activity numbers look like?
- ♦ How can we improve our upselling ratios?

THERE IS ANOTHER REASON telesales is a difficult job, but this one has to do with numbers, and it is completely within our control. Most telesales teams that I know of do not monitor their numbers in any meaningful way. I will tell you a secret about my training program. There is nothing that is easier to implement and more likely to generate a measurable increase in sales than the act of getting your team to measure their own numbers. Mind you, I am not talking about instituting some Orwellian scheme under which the managers spy on the salespeople and compile numbers independent from them. What I am talking about is changing the culture in such a way as to make the salespeople in any telesales team—or, indeed, in any selling team—conclude, of their own accord, that it makes sense for them to monitor their own numbers because they will make more money if they do.

Take a look at the following graphic.

Inbound Sales Number	discussions	interviews	proposals/ presentations	initial sales	upsell attempts	upsells
	100	81	74	40	11	1

Notice that these are numbers for an inbound selling team and that the numbers in question are for one sales rep. Monitoring inbound phone sales numbers is a good illustration, because it is in an inbound selling environment that we are also asked to upsell to the prospective customer who has called in to us. So think of the following numbers as though they were someone answering the telephone at a call center, perhaps in response to an infomercial advertising exercising equipment. The total number of sales would be one figure; the total number of upsales, namely, a subscription to a company's fitness magazine, might be another.

In this figure, we have 100 total discussions during the course of a day and 81 interviews. By interview, I mean an intelligent discussion with the person making the decision about whether or not to buy from us. This is a point at which we ask a key question that will help us to both gauge the person's interest and engage the other person in a conversation. Of course, as we pose questions, we are gathering information.

Those eighty-one interviews led to seventy-four proposals or presentations. That is to say, out of those eighty-one interviews, there were seventy-four times when the discussion led to a direct recommendation to buy the exercise equipment.

Of those seventy-four proposals, forty turned into sales. So a little more than half of the time, the inquiry about the exercise equipment turned into sales for us. Now watch what happens.

We make eleven upselling attempts in this scenario. Of those eleven upsell attempts, we find that one turns into an actual subscription. The point is that sales is a numerically driven process, built around the concept of *ratios*. These activity totals don't exist

Outbound Sales Number	call attempts	discussions	interviews	proposals/ presentations	initial sales	upsell attempts	upsells
	181	100	81	74	40	11	1

in a vacuum—they relate to one another, and their relationships are something we can measure.

That is true in the inbound selling environment, and it is also true for outbound sales as well. Take a look at the graphic.

Notice that the outbound call process starts with one column to the left of the "discussions" box, which adds another element to the equation. In this case, we might make, say, 181 calls in order to generate those 100 discussions.

My point is not that these numbers are right or wrong. My point is that they are interrelated. I do not know if forty sales is a good number for you or a bad number for you. All I know is, it takes seventy-four presentations or proposals to generate those forty initial sales. And I know, too, based on our scenario, that of those forty initial sales, we are making only eleven upsell attempts and, by the same token, we are closing only one sale for the magazine subscription. So, here is my question: How could we increase the total number of upsells?

If you spend any time at all looking at the numbers, you will realize where the opportunity lies. We look at the chart again, notice that we have closed forty initial sales, and we have made only eleven upsell attempts. Of those eleven, we closed one. Why on earth would we not make forty attempts to match the forty sales that we closed? If we did that, the ratio of our upsell attempts, one to eleven, would almost certainly stay in the same ballpark. Let's assume it stays exactly the same. Simply by asking the twenty-nine additional people about an upsell opportunity, we could add two and perhaps three additional upsells to our day . . . and increase our income measurably. How long would it take to close off *each* additional conversation with the same request about whether the person would like to subscribe to the fitness magazine?

Notice I am not asking at this point what form that request should take, only whether it makes sense to ask it at the end of every conversation in which we actually sell something. I hope you can see through this simple illustration that, in this case, it definitely does make sense to ask forty, not eleven, people whether they want to buy a subscription to our fitness magazine.

| CHAPTER 13 |

What Do the Numbers Mean?

If you don't quit, and don't cheat, and don't run home when trouble arrives, you can only win.

—SHELLEY LONG

- ◆ How do activity numbers relate to income?
- ◆ Where does the upselling ratio fit in with the rest of the activity?
- ◆ Why is it important for us to track our own numbers?
- ◆ How does setting a quota for daily activity relate to our overall sales quota?
- ◆ What does upselling look like in the outbound sales environment?

LET'S THINK FOR A MOMENT about what the numbers you just looked at in the last chapter could really mean to your career.

Imagine how they could change your relationship with your supervisor. Instead of offering vague advice like "you must do better" or "you have to close more sales," which only makes salespeople frustrated, imagine what would happen if you were able to track the total number of:

- • Calls
- • Sales interviews
- • Initial presentations/pitches/recommendations
- • Initial closed sales

- Upsell attempts
- Upsells

. . . and then strategize the improvements *you* wanted to see in your performance!

It's not enough for a manager simply to say, "You have to do better." It's not even enough for a salesperson to say to him- or herself, "I have to do better." Instead, we have to be willing to ask ourselves, exactly how many discussions with people does it take for me to reach my goal for a given day?

When we ask ourselves a question like, Exactly how many discussions with people does it take for me to reach my goal for a given day? that presumes that we have a goal for that day. Where did that goal come from? Well, ideally, it comes from our own income goal for our own lifestyle. In other words, our activity is directly related to our daily routine, and it's that daily routine that delivers our income, and it is in turn that income that will determine our lifestyle.

Nobody disagrees with me when I make these points in the abstract, but making them specific is sometimes a bit of a challenge. Often, when I talk to salespeople in their sales training programs, I'll ask them, "How many dials did you make today?" (Or, if I were approaching a telesales group, I might say, "How many inbound calls did you take yesterday?" or "How many outbound calls did you make yesterday?")

Very often, salespeople, whether inbound or outbound, simply won't know how many dials or discussions they took part in just twenty-four hours earlier. If you think about it, that's really amazing. We live in an era where people know their Social Security number, the mileage on their car, their telephone number, even the batting average of the guy who just made the All-Star team. But they don't know how many dials or conversations they had yesterday with the people who will end up paying their salary!

It's a critical question because so many of the salespeople I work with are dissatisfied with their income. In other words, they want their income level to match a certain expectation, and they're not sure why it doesn't. Well, the income is determined by the activity, and if you don't know what the activity is, you're not in a great position to change it for the better!

Let me tell you a little bit about what I do. I still sell every day. Every day that I'm not training, I'll pick up the phone fifteen times, I'll make seven dials, and I'll set one first appointment. (I know we're talking about telesales, which in most cases doesn't have anything to do with first appointments, but let me consider an example from my own life just so you can see how the numbers work.)

If I do that every day of the week—fifteen dials, seven conversations, one appointment—I'll have five new appointments every week, right?

But how many total appointments will I go to?

The actual number in my case is eight. I have five first appointments that I set—that's three appointments during the course of a week that are follow-up appointments with people that I've met at least once. My selling cycle plays out over a two- or three-visit process. So I do have to go back for follow-up visits.

So that means that, during the course of the average week, I'm going to go out to eight meetings. My closing ratio, which I monitor carefully, demonstrates to me that I will close one sale for every eight meetings that I go to. So that means that if I do my job, and I set my five new appointments and three follow-up appointments every week without fail, I will close one new deal each week. That's good for me—maybe not for you, but for me—because my goal is fifty total sales per year.

So here's the critical question: What is the total number of dials you should make? When I ask our participants in the sales training programs what their total number of dials is, I usually get a quizzical look and then perhaps a guess: "I don't know . . . six?" As though I know the answer and they don't.

I'll continue bravely and say, "Okay, let's assume it's six. Why that number?"

And again, the person stares at me as though I were asking him or her to recite the Magna Carta.

If someone were to ask me why I make my fifteen dials each and every day, I would know the answer to that question. I wouldn't stare back as though I were being interrogated by some surrealistic figure in a bad dream. I would have the answer. I make those fifteen dials every day *in order to* generate the seven discussions and the eight meetings every week. I generate the eight meetings every week *in order to* close one sale per week. I close the one sale per week *in order to* have fifty sales over the course of the year. And I want those fifty sales because that's my lifestyle number. That matches my income goal. I know for a fact that my activity is related to my performance.

So notice that, in my case, I have a series of ratios that affect the total income I eventually earn. *Dials, conversations, appointments, and sales.*

Now look again at that graphic that outlines the ratios of the inbound total sales performer. Those are ratios, too. We have a total number of calls, which relates to the number of sales discussions that arise. We have a total number of presentations or recommendations, which arises out of those sales discussions. We have a total number of closed sales, which is intimately related to the number of presentations we make. We have a total number of upsell attempts, which connects to the closed sales, and a total number of upsells that we actually close.

Here's my point. These numbers don't operate in a vacuum. And no, you can't simply expect your sales manager to track them for you. *You* have to track them for yourself, because it's *your* lifestyle that the numbers will determine!

You can't simply set a quota for the final element without setting a quota for the first element! Too many sales managers and salespeople focus only on the result—and not on the cause that will deliver their results.

The Outbound Side

We've seen what the ratios look like for inbound calls. What do they look like for outbound calls?

In this case, we want to track the total number of:

- Dials
- Completed calls
- Presentations, pitches, and recommendations
- Closed sales
- Upsells

In the outbound sales environment, upselling can happen in a couple of different ways. We can close the sale and sell our exercise equipment during the call and then follow up immediately with a request or a suggestion that the person buy a subscription to our magazine. Or we can follow up at a later point in time and suggest that the person consider subscribing to the magazine.

CHAPTER 14

Two Models

*You can have everything in life that you want if you just give
enough other people what they want.*

—Zig Ziglar

- ♦ What are the critical points in the inbound call sequence?
- ♦ What are the critical points in the outbound call sequence?
- ♦ What role do "objections" or negative responses play in the call?
- ♦ What should we do when we encounter them?
- ♦ What are some effective transitional phrases?

LET'S LOOK A LITTLE BIT at the dynamics under which the inbound
and outbound calls unfold. They are actually quite different—but
they are both focused on the task of developing a conversation that
will enable us to gather the information we need to help the other
person better *do* what he or she does.

The reason that they are so different is that the mindset of the
people whom we are talking to in the telesales situation is different.

Let's look at the inbound telesales call first. You're the caller;
I'm the salesperson. In an inbound sale, you have perhaps seen a
promotional piece or an infomercial, heard about my company from
a friend, or had some other source of information that led you to me.
So you pick up the telephone and you call. Usually, you will be calling with a very specific purpose in mind. In many selling situations,
the person who makes the inbound call will be trying to track down
a quote or get an idea of the general price range for a certain product
or service. In other words, they may not be ready to buy.

However, even if the person is not eager or willing to buy from us, he or she did initiate the call—and that makes a world of difference when it comes to strategizing the call from the salesperson's perspective. There are two critical points in the inbound selling model. Take a look at the steps in this model of a successful inbound sale:

1. Greeting/Hello
2. *Critical Point #1:* Segue to information-gathering phase
3. Interviewing or Information Gathering
4. *Critical Point #2:* Verification of information to close on presentation
5. Presentation or Plan
6. Close

Notice that the call opens with a greeting or some form of saying hello. After that, the first critical point is that we segue to the *information-gathering phase* of the call. We want to move out of the initial pleasantry phase and into the portion of the call where we are determining what is happening in the other person's world. So the transition out of the first element and into the second one is extremely important. The inbound call will usually stand or fall on the person's ability to make this transition.

The second critical point is the *verification phase.* This is where we confirm what we have learned about the other person and try to get the facts straight so that we can build our presentation around it. I should point out here that this presentation may take place during this call or during a subsequent call, but regardless of how many telephone conversations it takes for me to get to that point, I do have to verify my information if I want to have a chance to close the sale. You see that the presentation itself follows the verification, and the closing element follows that.

So you can see the two most critical elements of that call are the point at which we are able to move the person out of his or her immediate questions or opening pleasantries and into the information phase—and then whether we are able to confirm that the information that we have gotten really does reflect something that is happening in the other person's world.

The outbound call is quite different. In this situation, the other person is not expecting our call. In fact, he or she is doing something else entirely.

It will come as no surprise to you, I am sure, that the person we are calling not only does not expect the call, but even has a negative response all ready for us when we make it. In other words, we call our prospect at 11:30 in the morning, and he is preparing for a big meeting that he has to attend at 12:00. Guess what? Talking to us about our widget is the last thing on his mind. So this call has a different first critical point—it's the part where the person we're calling tells us, in one way or another, that he's really not interested in pursuing the conversation. Take a look at the steps in the outbound sales model:

1. Greeting/Hello
2. *Critical Point #1:* Getting past initial negative response
3. Interviewing or Information Gathering
4. *Critical Point #2:* Verifying of information to close on presentation
5. Presentation or Plan
6. Close

That initial negative response is virtually always waiting for us when we place an outbound telesales call. It does not matter whether our widgets are the best thing on the planet, our price is the most competitive, or even whether the person has just been given the formal responsibility to track down widgets for the organization. The urge to get ready for that meeting (or to do whatever the person was doing before we called) means we are going to hear the negative response.

The response is typically something along the lines of "I'm not interested" or "I don't have time for this."

It is not a reasoned, intellectual response to what we've said. It is more like a knee-jerk response.

So getting past that initial response is obviously the very first critical point here. If we do not find some way to turn that response around and develop some kind of conversation, nothing is going to happen during this call.

The second critical point is the same as in the inbound. In this situation, we also want to verify the information so we can close our presentation.

At this point, I want to challenge you to think of these two models as the means by which we can get to a basic or simple sale. In other words, think about these two models, with their two critical points, as the work that you need to do to get on the other person's radar screen and turn him or her from a prospect into a customer.

To do this, we'll use a calling approach, which might sound like the following in the inbound environment:

> ***Greeting/ID self and company:*** "Thank you for calling ABC Widget."

> ***Get basic information from caller:*** "Can I get your name and phone number, please?"
> "Thank you!"
> "And could I take down your address, too?"
> "Great! And what can I do for you today?"

> ***Transition to information gathering (What has CHANGED in the person's world?):*** "By the way, can I ask you what made you decide to call us today?"

And here's what the approach might look like in the outbound mode:

> ***Attention statement:*** "Hi, Mr. Jones."

> ***ID self and company:*** "This is Brian Marks from ABC Company. I'm not sure if you're familiar with us—we're the biggest supplier of widgets on the East Coast."

> ***Reason for the call, built around a BENEFIT:*** "The reason I'm calling you specifically today is that we've been working with a lot of (homeowners/your counterparts in the _____ industry/companies in the _____ area) to help them reduce their widget expenses."

Transition to information gathering: "Just out of curiosity, what are you doing now to maintain your widgets?"

And we'll prepare and practice a turnaround, which might sound like this:

Turnaround: "You know, some of our best customers told us that before they saw how we could improve their bottom line. Just out of curiosity, have you ever worked with a widget reconditioning service before? *(Any response.)* I see . . . well, that's why we really *should* be talking, because we've helped a lot of people in your situation. Would it help if I told you a little bit about what we do?" (An extremely *brief* ten- to thirty-second commercial follows, permitting you to pose another question and continue gathering information.)

Then we'll interview for information, using *do*-based questions. We'll replay what we've learned, and we'll verify our information. Then, God willing, we'll close the sale by saying, "Gee, based on what you're telling me, this really makes sense to me. What do you think?"

The question for us then is, how do we get the person to buy more?

"By the Way"

Three simple words will not only help you upsell, but will also help you to manage *all* the transitions you just saw in those two sales models, the inbound and the outbound. The words are: *"By the way . . ."*

There is a variation on this phrase that is almost as effective. It sounds like this: *"Just out of curiosity . . ."*

These are known as transitional phrases, and you should practice using them until they become second nature. Let's see how the phrases can help you to manage these four critical points in the telesales dialogue.

Take the inbound call first. You will remember what I said earlier in the book. Let's reinforce a key point here, namely, that information is what makes effective selling possible. If I do not have the right information, then I am not going to be able to connect with this person on anything more than a superficial level. If I do not have the right information, I can expect to get only the sales that "drop into your lap"—the sales that were going to happen anyway. My skill as a salesperson will not come into play when it comes to my developing a relationship with this prospect.

So what is the most important piece of information that I want to find out about the person who is placing the inbound call to me or my company? Take a moment and think about the answer to that question. Please do not move on to the next chapter until you have come up with an answer.

CHAPTER 15

What You Really Want to Know

Champions keep playing until they get it right.
—BILLIE JEAN KING

- What's the most important piece of information you should be trying to uncover on an inbound call?
- When should we ask about this?
- What should our question sound like?
- How can we use "by the way" and "just out of curiosity" to uncover this information?

DID YOU ACTUALLY come up with an answer . . . or did you simply turn the page? There is no penalty for cheating—but bear in mind that you will get the most out of this book if you make a conscious decision to *change what isn't working and replace it with something that does work.* So you should, at the very least, identify what you're trying to find out from people over the telephone right now and compare it with what I'm going to suggest that you try to find out from this point forward.

Pretend I'm the telesales representative, and I'm taking an inbound call. My information-gathering priority is *finding out what made the person decide to call me in the first place.*

This is an extremely important principle, one that I hope you will build into each and every calling day.

"By the way, what made you decide to call us today?"
"By the way, can I ask how you heard about us?"

Or, if the person "knows" he "needs" widgets:

"Just out of curiosity, what made you decide you needed to order widgets?"

Or:

"Just out of curiosity, what made you choose to call us about this?"

By identifying exactly what made the person decide to get in touch with us, we do a couple of very important things. We start to uncover what's going on in the other person's world, and we make it clear that our job as a salesperson is to find out about the other person.

The caller could say to me that his equipment just broke down or that his sales force has just had a huge increase in quarterly sales targets. He could say to me that he is pricing a number of different vendors in order to arrange for a presentation to his own CEO. He could tell me that his standard training vendor has canceled unexpectedly, and he is looking for a replacement for this Monday morning at 8:30. These are all very different situations.

Whatever the answer that comes back to me sounds like, I am going to find some way to place it in the context of what my organization has done before. So if the person is calling because the sales training company backed out at the last minute, I can share a number of stories that illustrate how we have been able to come through in similar situations for some of our clients. We have found many ways to build long-term relationships with such "accidental" customers.

Look at it again:

"Just out of curiosity, what made you decide to get in contact with us today?"

You must—repeat, *must*—ask the other person at some point very early in the conversation *exactly what prompted his or her call.*

CHAPTER 16

"My Hands Are Tied!"

Ah, but a man's reach should exceed his grasp, or what's a heaven for?

—Robert Browning

- ♦ What if our opening words during the inbound call must match a script we've been given?
- ♦ How does working to uncover the reason for the inbound caller's call affect our mindset?
- ♦ How does it affect our upselling efforts?

It really is imperative that you make an effort to learn what made an inbound caller decide to get in touch with your organization. If you are a telesales professional and you're hoping to use this book to improve your upselling numbers, rest assured that this one simple step is the single most important piece of advice you're going to read in this book. If you do this, you *will* gather more and better information, and you'll be in a great position to improve your upselling totals.

The *mindset* you bring to this undertaking is all-important. If you believe you are constrained by the requirements of your manager, your script, your employer, the economy, or any other force outside yourself, you will have already lost most of the battle. The trick is to take whatever structure you're working under and *turn it toward* the task of learning what has changed in this person's life.

Sometimes I will work with salespeople who say, "Steve, I'd like to ask why the person decided to call us—what's different in his or her world, what made him decide to call me rather than go bowling or something. You're right. I should know that. But my hands are tied! They give me a script, and I have to follow it. When I answer the phone, I have to say the words, 'Hi, this is Jim Miller, thank you for calling ABC Company. How can I help you?'"

I always tell them, "Fine . . . so go ahead and say that. But then, at the very first opportunity, once you have found a way to deliver the opening portion the way you are supposed to, you should also find a way to get to the bottom of a very basic human question: How come you did this? Why did you decide to get in touch with us? What prompted your call?"

There are probably a dozen different ways you could phrase this all-important question. In the final analysis, it really does not matter how it is phrased, as long as it *is* phrased, and as long as it is comfortable for you. I have used the two phrases "by the way" and "just out of curiosity" in this book because these phrases have been proven to deliver good results for most of the people we train.

In case you had not noticed, the opening question, "What made you decide to call us today?" is, in fact, a relatively simple transition out of the opening portion of the call and into the information-gathering phase. We are asking an intelligent question about what the person does, and we are going to continue asking intelligent questions to follow up on our query about what made the person decide to call. As a result, we are going to be working from a much better platform when the time comes to upsell. We're going to have developed much more meaningful information than will the salesperson who *doesn't* know what has recently changed in the prospect's world.

CHAPTER 17

The Turnaround in Action

For me, winning isn't something that happens suddenly on the field when the whistle blows and the crowds roar. Winning is something that builds physically and mentally every day that you train and every night that you dream.
　　　　　　　　　　—EMMITT SMITH, NFL RUNNING BACK

- ♦ How does the outbound call sound?
- ♦ What role does the initial negative response play in the outbound call?
- ♦ How can we get past that negative response and move into the information-gathering phase?

You've seen how to establish the right platform—the information-based platform—to prepare for upselling on the inbound call. What about on the outbound call?

We've already seen that the initial negative response is the first critical point in the outbound call. Take a look at this opening to an outbound call, and see how it matches up with our goal of getting past the person's initial negative response.

> *Telephone: Ring, ring.*
> *Prospect:* "Mike Miller here."
> *Me:* "Mike Miller?"
> *Prospect:* "Yes."
> *Me:* "Steven Schiffman here from D.E.I. Management Group. I'm not sure whether you've heard of us, but we're

one of the largest sales training companies in the country. We've done a lot of work with companies in your industry, like ABC, 123, and XYZ. The reason I'm calling you today specifically is that we've just finished working on a program for . . ."

Prospect: "Let me stop you right there, Steve. I have absolutely no interest in talking to you this afternoon."

(Here comes our turnaround . . . remember that our goal is to get into the information-gathering portion of the conversation.)

Me: "You know, it's funny you should mention that. We have a lot of situations where we hear that. In fact, I can't tell you the number of people who've said that to me and then ended up working with us. By the way . . . have you ever worked with a widget company before?"

Notice that I have used a very simple turnaround that validates the person's objection and allows me to regain control of the conversation through using the phrase "by the way." I have said, basically, "Yeah, I hear what you are saying, and that is a very common piece of feedback for me. I hear that a lot." Then immediately after that, I pose a question of my own.

I don't ask just any question, but a question that allows me to start gathering important information. I want to maintain control of the call, and I want, if possible, to learn something interesting about this person. So, in this case, it is entirely possible that I could get past both critical points at the same time. I am going to ask a question that is designed to reveal a very important piece of information, namely, whether or not the company has ever worked with a company like mine before. It is possible that the answer is yes; it is possible that the answer is no. In either case, I am going to assume that I can provide some type of anecdote or story that supports my company and justifies continuing with the discussion.

Take a look at that turnaround again. Here it is phrased in a slightly different way:

Prospect: "Steve, let me stop you right there. We have absolutely no interest in speaking to a sales trainer at this point in time."

Me: "Okay, I hear you. And to tell you the truth, we do get that a lot. Even some of the people who end up working with us said initially that they really had no interest in talking to us. Just out of curiosity, have you ever worked with a sales training company before?"

This is a classic do-based question, one that can help us to identify precisely where the person is in regard to using our products or service. If I were selling exercise equipment, the question might sound like this: "By the way, have you ever purchased an exercise program before?"

If I were selling newspaper subscriptions, it might sound like this: "By the way, are you taking any newspapers right now?"

It is entirely possible, of course, that the person will throw a new objection my way, perhaps one that has absolutely nothing whatsoever to do with the one that I just heard. That is the way it is early on in the discussion. The first thing you hear, someone says to you, "I have no interest, I have never had any interest, and you know what? I will never be interested as long as I live." Then thirty seconds later, you get another objection from the same person and it sounds like this: "I have no budget. We did it last year, but now I don't have any money."

What happened to the fact that they had no interest whatsoever for the rest of their lives? And they never did this before? That was the implication of that first objection; the second makes it a little bit clearer that something did happen at some point in the past. The key is not to let the initial negative responses turn you off. They are only instinctive, reflex responses. You do not want to give them too much credence, and you do not want to ignore them. You want to validate them. And then you want to ask a question of your own.

This is an extremely compressed version of the turnaround process that I suggest in my full-scale training program. For more information on how to handle turnarounds in a sales call, I suggest you take a look at my books, *Telesales* and *Cold Calling Techniques (That Really Work!)*.

CHAPTER 18

Another Use for "By the Way"

Many men go fishing all of their lives without knowing that it is not fish they are after.

—HENRY DAVID THOREAU

- How can we use transitional phrases to help verify our information?
- What can the verification substep sound like?
- Is the verification substep short or long?

You have seen how you can use the simple "by the way" or just "I'm just curious" phrases to get past the initial response, to develop a meaningful conversation, and to start moving into the information-gathering process. You can also use these phrases to verify your information. It might sound like this:

"So what I'm getting from you is that A, B, and C are important to you. By the way, a lot of our clients think D is important as well. Is that an issue for you, or have we covered everything with A, B, and C?"

This is a classic verification question, one that is likely to be used in a telesales call where the sales process is relatively short. We are just replaying what we have learned from the conversation and then adding that, by the way, the person's counterpart at such and such an organization or such and such an industry has experienced some other element as well. Does what the counterpart experienced match what the prospect has experienced, or do we need any more information?

Obviously, in more complex sales, the verification process can go into considerably more depth. I have worked in industries where the selling cycle is a year and a half to two years long! In those situations, verification becomes an extremely important and lengthy part of the sales process that usually involves several salespeople and technical experts at the same time.

The point is that you cannot simply move forward to offer your presentation until *you have confirmed or verified your information.* If that means the conversation continues for a while, so be it! Go into as much depth as you can with the customer. As long as you're uncovering relevant information and the person is invested, as you are, in the process of moving the sale forward, keep asking questions and verifying what you've learned. Remember, you are supposed to do 75 percent of your work *before* you make a formal recommendation or suggest a specific plan.

CHAPTER 19

The Telesales Upsell

Education is what survives when what has been learned has been forgotten.

—B. F. Skinner

- ♦ What does the telesales upsell sound like?
- ♦ What roles do habit and repetition play in the upselling process?
- ♦ How should we close the sale?
- ♦ How does "by the way" help us move into the upselling phase?
- ♦ What are the two possible philosophies for telesales success?

WE CAN ALSO USE THE "BY THE WAY" PHRASE as a strategy for upselling during the call. And it is this use of the phrase that we must be absolutely certain to turn into a habit—because it is only by making a regular habit of what I call the "by the way" upsell strategy, that we can make significant improvement in our numbers.

If we only know that we *should* ask for additional business, but fail to do so, we're wasting our time and our company's investment in us as salespeople!

Let's say that the person has agreed to purchase the exercise equipment from us that we wanted to talk about. This can happen both as a result of an inbound call to us, or as a result of our call to the person, based on his or her having called us in the past or sent in a request of some kind. In any event, assume we have closed the sale by gathering the right information, verifying it, and then saying something along the lines of, "It makes sense to me—what do you think?"

So, at this point, the person is going to purchase our (for instance) exercise equipment. He or she has given us the credit card information and has confirmed all of the details for the order.

Before we close out the call, however, it is very important for us to make some kind of an upselling attempt, assuming that is something that is supported by our product or service offering. Usually it is.

Here, in my perfect world, is what that upselling effort sounds like. Notice how simple it is!

"By the way, Mrs. Jones, we have a special on today for people who order the Power Riser Ab Cruncher exercise unit. If you wanted to, you could get our award-winning magazine, *Abs on Parade,* for just $9.95 today—it's usually $19.95. Should I put you down for that?"

Notice that the phrase "by the way" inoculates us against any sensation that we may be pressuring the person too much. If used properly, this phrase makes everything we say sound conversational and relevant to the person's situation. We are not pressuring, we are not pushing, we are just mentioning something of interest. By the way, we also have this special on.

If you are not comfortable with "by the way" or you are already using it and do not want to keep repeating it over and over, you could say something like this:

"Just out of curiosity, Mr. Jones, we do have a special on today for people who order the unit that you have asked to have delivered. Our award-winning magazine, *Abs on Parade,* usually costs $19.95, but because you ordered the unit from us today, you would be able to get it for half off, only $9.95. The magazine shows you a lot of advanced exercises you can use in developing your muscles. Should I go ahead and lock in that low rate for you?"

Remember—if you don't ask, you don't sell!

Similar to the "by the way" opening, the "just out of curiosity" opening makes the upsell sound casual and conversational. The tone is just as important as the words you say. Keep it light, keep it human, keep it personal—and do not close the call without offering some variation on the phrases "by the way" or "just out of curiosity" in reference to an upselling offer that your company extends.

Two Basic Telesales Philosophies

In telesales, there are two basic selling (and, by extension, upselling) philosophies. It is up to us to choose which one is right for our market situation. If we choose the wrong philosophy for the situation in which we find ourselves selling, we have only ourselves to blame.

- Philosophy #1: *Speak to as many different people as possible.*
- Philosophy #2: *Spend as much time with each person as possible.*

This is an extremely important but typically overlooked point about selling on the phone. Your telesales approach must reflect the right philosophy!

Identify which basic approach is more likely to lead to success in your business situation.

Here is the key question: How much information do you need?

If you need a large amount of information, you may need to spend as much time with each person as possible—and make plenty of follow-through calls to check in on the person's status, gather and confirm new information, and make additional "by the way" upselling appeals, based on your relationship with that specific customer.

If, on the other hand, you need a comparatively small amount of information, you will probably want to pile up as many contacts as possible and probably make your upselling attempt at the conclusion of the call that terminates in a sale.

It is *your* job, as a telesales professional, to determine which philosophy is right for you.

CHAPTER 20

Additional Thoughts on the Telesales Upselling Process

Don't tell people how to do things, tell them what to do and let them surprise you with their results.

—GEORGE S. PATTON

- ♦ What are the keys to upselling success over the phone?
- ♦ What role does tonality play?
- ♦ What is the right emotional message to send over the phone?
- ♦ What role do success stories play?
- ♦ What role does humor play?

FOR ME, upselling over the phone is basically built around an individual salesperson's creativity *and* the words "by the way. . . ."

We have already gotten something going with the person, and we know that we have that business. Before we imagine that the relationship is complete, we take advantage of the fact that we have built up a certain comfort level with the person, and we keep that casual tone going by saying, "By the way, we have this other thing you might be interested in. . . ." And we build the conversation creatively from there.

I want to share with you a few additional theories and concepts about upselling in the telesales environment. These are some concepts that will, I think, help you as you work to develop and expand your relationships with prospective customers.

First and foremost, remember that the *emotional tone* you set in the first few seconds of the call is extremely important to your upselling efforts. What you say—and how you say it—will have a tremendous positive or negative effect on the rapport you are able to build with your contact. So, be absolutely sure you do not sound as though you wish you were someplace else while making your calls.

Instead, send the message, both with words and in tonality, that you are having a great day, that you love what you do for a living, that any job worth doing is worth doing well, and that you are capable of taking good care of people that come into your life. These are all important messages that can be "said" in the very first few moments, indeed the first few seconds of your call. I have had calls with telesales professionals who communicated all these positive messages simply by means of a single word—*hello*—and saying their name. If you say your name with pride, with energy, and with optimism, you will go a long way toward establishing rapport with your prospective customer.

In addition, I believe you should identify and become comfortable discussing at least ten relevant success stories: These are important because you need to be able to give examples of how what your company does has benefited other people. Consider ten as a bare minimum. Learn them, become conversant with their details, and be ready to share their specifics—with enthusiasm—at a moment's notice.

Finally, be willing to use appropriate humor to lighten the mood of the call: it is possible to turn a difficult call around if you know how to use self-deprecating humor. If you can keep your poise and laugh your way through an awkward moment, you will be well on your way to establishing the one-on-one vocal rapport that makes selling—and upselling—over the phone possible.

There is a great deal more to be said about upselling over the phone—most of it, however, overlaps with the best strategies and processes of face-to-face upselling. So please do continue with Part III of this book, even if you think it might not apply to you.

Part III

Face-to-Face

CHAPTER 21

Questions You Should Be Able to Answer

I dread success. To have succeeded is to have finished one's business on earth, like the male spider, who is killed by the female the moment he has succeeded in his courtship. I like a state of continual becoming, with a goal in front and not behind.

—GEORGE BERNARD SHAW

♦ What questions about the customer should we be ready to answer *before* we attempt to close a sale or upsell?
♦ What questions about ourselves and our company should we be ready to answer *before* we attempt to close a sale or upsell?

GATHERING INFORMATION IS A PROCESS that never really ends but that can, in my experience, at least be initiated properly.

Here are some of the questions I try to make sure salespeople can answer *before* they attempt to close the deal or upsell:

1. When are you going back?
2. *(If talking to a company)* What does the company do, and who are its customers?
3. Who are you talking to?
4. Why that person?
5. *(If talking to a company)* How long has your contact been there for?

6. *(If talking to a company)* What is this company doing now in an area where we can add value? And why aren't they using us already?
7. When was the first meeting or conversation?
8. Did you call them or did they call you?
9. How much is the deal worth?
10. In your view, what is the very next thing that has to happen for you to eventually close this sale?
11. When and how will you make that happen?
12. Who else are they looking at?
13. Why them?
14. What does your contact think is going to happen next?
15. When is that going to happen?
16. Do they want this deal to happen as much as you do?
17. What is your customer trying to do or accomplish?

And here are some additional "introspective" questions that I would encourage you to consider: The first seven are particularly important; their answers should be developed carefully, reviewed, shared with others, and rehearsed over and over again.

1. What do we sell?
2. What makes us unique?
3. What makes us better than the competition?
4. *(Complete the sentence)* Even though our cost may be higher, people buy from us because . . .
5. Why do you work for this company?
6. How will you create the flow? (That is, what question will you ask to initiate the next conversation?)
7. What is your Next Step strategy? (See Chapter 32.)
8. If you could ask any question of your typical contacts, what would it be?
9. What information could you gather that would either increase the speed of your sales cycle or improve your closing ratio?
10. If you reached out to someone besides your typical contact, what else could you ask and what else could you learn?

11. How many initial discussions does it take you to develop a prospect? (For "prospect," think "Someone with whom I have had at least two good conversations and who is willing to set a time to talk to me again."
12. How many prospects does it take you to generate a sale?
13. How many upselling attempts does it take you to generate an upsell?

CHAPTER 22

Four Phases
of the Relationship

It is one of the most beautiful compensations of this life that no man can sincerely try to help another without helping himself.

—RALPH WALDO EMERSON

♦ What is the *seller* phase of the relationship between buyer and seller?

♦ What is the *supplier* phase of the relationship between buyer and seller?

♦ What is the *vendor* phase of the relationship between buyer and seller?

♦ What is the *partner/resource* phase of the relationship between buyer and seller?

♦ How do these four phases relate to what is happening in the Upselling Pyramid?

SOMETIMES, we think of our upselling efforts as though they exist in a vacuum or as though they are being made with customers who are all identical. Actually, any attempt to move with a customer to a decision to purchase additional goods and services from us moves through a continuum. We can chart that continuum by looking closely at the level of the relationship that we have been able to develop with this person.

Let's look at first from the point of view of our customer. From the customer's point of view, we are likely to fall into one of the following four categories:

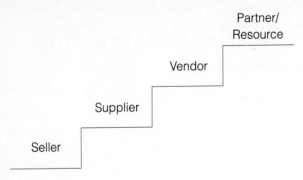

From the customer's point of view, there are four levels on the sales continuum. What we notice as salespeople is that the higher we move with the person on this four-step continuum, the better our information gets and the more valuable the relationship becomes.

At the lowest level, the customer simply considers us to be a *seller.* At this level, we have virtually no trust or information. The customer thinks of us typically as a onetime provider, and we may have that same mentality on our side. Most of the sales that "fall into your lap" come under the category of the low-level, seller relationship.

If we were to move up a little bit on the scale, the customer would consider us to be a *supplier.* The supplier relationship features a fair amount of trust and information, but not a great deal. Basically, you're "in the Rolodex" when somebody considers you a supplier. When people look at what we offer this way, upselling is a possibility but not a sure thing. The customer may decide to contact us. We may decide to contact the customer. But in either event, there is a certain "prove it to me" mindset that must be overcome before the relationship gets particularly meaningful for either party.

The third level of connection is called the *vendor* level. When a customer thinks of us as a vendor, the relationship is marked by significant levels of trust and information. There is actually predictable repeat business here, and many people make the mistake of assuming that, if you upsell to a person regularly and you reach this level, you have hit the highest level possible. It's not at all true.

At the highest level is a *partner/resource* relationship. Here there are extremely high levels of trust and information and you function as a strategic partner/resource, and you and the customer are mutually dependent on each other for success. At the partner/resource level, you have easy access to all key players within the organization.

The Upselling Pyramid

You've seen how the customer perceives us, and the four steps in the relationship.

Now, we have a few more detailed ways of looking at this same process when we break it down from the point of view of the salesperson. Notice that the following pyramid encompasses all of the steps you just saw.

Here's what each of these levels tells you in regard to the type of relationship you have with the customer and how likely you are to be able to upsell with them:

Strategic Relationship

"Matching vision, values, mission and ethics"—Positioning your company here sets you apart from the competition, makes upselling easy, and makes the relationship difficult to duplicate.

Strategic Supplier

"We help businesses do more business"—Upselling is comparatively easy here. By helping the prospect fulfill key objectives, we really begin to differentiate ourselves over time.

Future Direction

Your company emerges as a leader, with solid service and reliability. Upselling is a 50/50 proposition. The prospect looks to narrow the field of competitors here.

Product and Features

Feature, functionality, service quality, and application to fit are the big issues here. Upselling is not an issue, nor is it likely. If the prospect's decision is based on nothing higher than price and features, the competition may win this sale from us. If we win this sale, the competition may win the next sale with little difficulty.

Price: Commodity Market

Everybody is in the game here. The winner may not be your company. Upselling is not a realistic possibility, as future purchases are probably not on the prospect's radar screen.

Can you see that if you hit the top level, or even are moving toward it from the second or third level from the top, then it is impossible for you to be at any of those levels *without knowing why the person decided to work with you?*

In other words, if you really understand the strategic purpose of the company and you understand the vision and you understand the major goals, you must, by definition, understand why the person is writing a check for you. You must understand where you add value. You must understand where, precisely, you help the company to achieve its goals and fulfill its mission.

The closer we get to the strategic vision and the further we move away from a commodity sale, the more likely we are to be able to understand the most important motivating factors behind the person's decision to buy from us. And the better we understand that, the easier it is to work with the person to expand the relationship.

| CHAPTER 23 |

Beware of Bad Assumptions

"There is no use trying," said Alice; "one can't believe impossible things."

"I dare say you haven't had much practice," said the Queen. "When I was your age, I always did it for half an hour a day. Why, sometimes I've believed as many as six impossible things before breakfast."

—LEWIS CARROLL, *THROUGH THE LOOKING GLASS*

♦ How might we mislead ourselves in our upselling efforts?
♦ What questions can we ask that will help us to overcome bad assumptions?
♦ How can we expect different people in the organization to respond to our questions?

A NATIONAL SALES MANAGER I KNOW was trying to expand his presence in one of his biggest accounts. He was not particularly successful, and he wanted my help in figuring out exactly why.

I asked him, "What are you selling them specifically?"

He said, "Well, among other things, paper—reams of business stock for use in copiers and printers."

I said, "Okay, how many people in the organization use paper?"

"Well," he said, "there are probably 15,000 people who use it, but there are only about 400 different work groups."

"Okay," I said. "There are 400 different work groups. How many of them are you talking to?"

"How many?" he asked.

"Yeah," I said. "How many of those 400 work groups are you in contact with?"

He went on to explain to me that he was "pretty certain" that they all bought through a single channel—namely, his channel. "That, at any rate," he said, "is my assumption."

I asked, "Why are you so certain of that?"

There was a long pause.

"I'll tell you one thing," I said. "If I had a company with 15,000 people using paper, I sure as heck wouldn't be channeling every single solitary purchase decision through one guy. My guess is that there are a lot more channels where paper is being sold than you're taking into account here. Have you ever asked them how they acquire their paper for those 15,000 people and those 400 work groups?"

"Well, no," he said.

We all can fall into this trap. We want to *assume* that the guy that we are talking to really is the guy who controls everything. We want to assume that the way that we have established a relationship really is the most efficient way to interact with our prospects. We want to assume that the work that we have done up front really is the only relevant work for us to do. But, in so many cases, those assumptions simply are not warranted.

The one thing that you can be sure about, especially in a major account, is that there is something going on behind the scenes that you can find out more about. So, in their situation, my instincts would be to go in to my contact or to somebody else within the organization and ask, "Just so I can be clear . . . how exactly do you acquire paper for your 400 work groups and your 15,000 people?"

That is the kind of question that a CEO or a senior executive will usually answer with confidence and authority and complete forthrightness in about a tenth of a second. By the same token, it is the kind of question that somebody who is placed a little bit lower on the chain of command would probably avoid, or he or she might spend forty-five minutes describing your terms back to you. So, sometimes, you have to reach out to other people in the organization.

When in doubt, ask, "Hey, how do you guys do X? Why do you do it that way?"

| CHAPTER 24 |

Raise the Hard Issues Yourself

People are like stained-glass windows. They sparkle and shine when the sun is out, but when the darkness sets in, their true beauty is revealed only if there is a light from within.
— ELIZABETH KÜBLER-ROSS

♦ How can we handle the most difficult objections or negative responses?
♦ What can we do to move the upselling process forward?
♦ How can we avoid hearing those dreaded words, "Let me think about it?"

WHEN I AM TRYING to move closer to the top of that Upselling Pyramid, trying to expand my relationship with a customer, I make a habit of identifying what I think the most difficult challenge in the relationship is going to be—and then bringing that problem up on my own, rather than waiting for the other person to do it.

You read right. What I do is try to put myself in the shoes of the other person, figure out what he or she would most likely object to in what I am proposing, and then talk about it first. Recall what I said a little bit earlier in this book about the art of being more concerned about something than the prospect or customer is. This is exactly what you should do when you have an upselling initiative—any upselling initiative—that you feel could conceivably carry a problem for the person you are talking to. Your goals should be to say something along the following lines:

- "I'll tell you the truth. I am actually kind of concerned about the price. I am not sure it is right. What do you think?"
- "To be honest with you, I am a little concerned that the program might not be focused on the most important topics for your people. What do you think?"
- "Here is where it fits together, but I have to be honest with you, I am a little bit concerned about how the schedule could work. I do not know if it is going to work for your organization."
- "Here is the piece that we are not certain about. We are trying to find out whether or not this payment plan is right for your family. Help me out. What do you think are the pros and cons?"
- "Let me tell you what is keeping me up at night. I think I understand what you are trying to accomplish here, and I think we can do it within your timeline. But I am not entirely sure that it is something you feel comfortable trying to share internally with your people, and I want to be sure that I get it right—help me out."

Whatever it is we are trying to sell more of—a piece of equipment, a series of training programs, a newspaper subscription, whatever—we should identify a particular problem that could be waiting for us around the corner somewhere. We then try to raise that tough issue ourselves rather than wait for the customer to do so.

After all, what is the alternative? If we know we are going to get hammered on price but we do not have any meaningful feedback about what price the other person is looking for, why on earth would we wait for the person to give us an objection—or even worse, an objection that is not truly an objection that still stalls the sale completely? You know the response I am talking about:

"Gee this is interesting, let me think about it."

I will do just about anything to avoid "Let me think about it." When it comes right down to it, I would much rather understand the true dimensions of the problem that is keeping the other person from deciding to buy more from me. I would rather get that information straight than hear some vague brush-off about needing more time to think about it or having to talk to somebody else.

By raising the most difficult issue ourselves and not waiting for the prospect to either bring it up or, even worse, fail to bring it up, we get a much better sense of exactly where we stand when it comes to the initiative of getting this person to buy more from us.

CHAPTER 25

Returning to the Plan

Management is doing things right; leadership is doing the right things.

—Peter F. Drucker

- What are the actual reasons behind a given customer's decision to buy from us?
- How do decision makers in seemingly identical situations differ in their motives for buying?
- What should our "compass" be in developing an upselling strategy for our customers?

Each and every person who has bought from us did so because it made sense for him or her to buy at that point in time—because our organization laid out a plan that connected to his or her interests. But here's the flip side of that (seemingly obvious) fact: People who *don't* buy from us again usually *decide* not to buy from us again because of our failure to follow through on the plan we laid out to them originally.

Whether we were aware of it or not, and sometimes we're not particularly aware, there is always some kind of plan or reason that guides these decisions of people who decide to buy from us. That initial plan or reason should be our compass in any upselling initiative.

Let's take the example of someone who purchases sales training from my company. You might think, if you're not particularly familiar with the sales training industry, that the only plan or reason that would guide someone to purchase sales training is the desire to increase sales. The truth, however, is a little more complex.

I really can't assume that each and every person to whom I speak during the course of the year is, in fact, simply interested in increasing sales. Sometimes people work with us because the actual plan or reason is usually a good deal more personal than that, and increasing sales may be only part of the picture or may not enter the equation at all.

Consider the case of someone who has recently inherited responsibility for a training department, a department that has been using our company to deliver its training for the past six years, with good results. Now, this new person has been told that he or she is responsible for selecting the training vendors—or even for eliminating the training budget entirely, if he or she chooses.

The actual circumstances are likely to vary, but in this situation, it's quite possible that the driving plan, or reason, for a decision to work with my company is not simply to increase sales, but to avoid changing a model that is already working, and sidestep or avoid entirely any problems with morale or performance that can be attributed to this new decision maker. In other words, he or she is very likely to want to avoid being held personally responsible for any change in the training regimen. That's a very different personal objective for a decision maker than simply wanting to increase sales.

If the person's job is dependent on his or her performance during the first year—which is not an uncommon circumstance—it's entirely possible that this person would completely overlook sales training in order to avoid the perception that he or she had advocated for something new and changed "what was already working."

I'm not saying that everyone would make a decision in this way, but that one should expect to run into certain decision makers who approach the issue in this way (and indeed we do). For such people, the objective is to avoid rocking the boat, to ensure continuity, and to avoid spending internal political capital they may need for other initiatives within the organization.

This is just one example of a situation where the perceived benefit of the product or service—increased sales—wouldn't necessarily match up with the actual plan or reason that the person might use to justify a purchase decision.

I'm not trying to be cynical about the underlying reasons to purchase sales training, but rather to give you a sense of the importance of identifying the *individual's* plan or reason for deciding to do business with you. We cannot assume that that plan or reason revolves around our own preconceptions; we must do the work necessary to *identify what was originally most important to this decision maker.*

And as long as that decision maker remains in the same place, is facing the same situation, and is focusing on the same goals, that plan or reason is what should drive our efforts to retain and upsell to the customer.

CHAPTER 26

The Six Mindsets
of Change

Finish each day and be done with it. You have done what you could. Some blunders and absurdities no doubt crept in; forget them as soon as you can. Tomorrow is a new day; begin it well and serenely and with too high a spirit to be encumbered with your old nonsense.

—RALPH WALDO EMERSON

♦ How do human beings approach the prospect of change?
♦ How do their attitudes evolve over time to a given change?
♦ What are the phases our customers are likely to go through?

HAVE YOU EVER NOTICED that some customers keep doing things in an old, inefficient way, even though they "know" there's a better way of approaching the task in question?

Why does that happen?

In order to facilitate constructive change for a person or an organization, you have to know where people are to begin with. Simply demanding that someone "do it the new way" will often make the situation worse.

Here's why. Change happens in certain predictable stages. Any time we human beings are challenged to develop a brand-new skill set, we are unlikely to adopt it instantly. To the contrary, we are likely to go through a developmental process with six distinct mindsets.

Mindset #1: Immobilization

We simply don't know what to do—and we are frozen in place. Typically, in this mindset, we say things like, "I don't believe in doing X. It just doesn't work for me." We don't even address the issue of whether change is in order. When dealing with people who are at this stage, it's a good idea to begin discussions with questions they will not perceive as threatening or attacking: "Why do you say that?" or "What makes you feel that way?" When we're in this mindset ourselves, we need support from other people.

Mindset #2: Denial (false competence)

We actively deny that any new approach is necessary. We try to improvise our way "around" the problem or pretend that we have skills that we don't. Typically, in this mindset, we say things like, "It sounds interesting, but the way I'm doing it now works for me." When dealing with people who are at this stage, it's a good idea to begin discussions with an analysis of what their current activities will actually deliver if they keep doing what they're doing. When we're in this mindset, we need evidence that it's time to make a change.

Mindset #3: Incompetence

We encounter serious problems in absence of the skill. Typically, in this mindset, we say things like, "Yikes—I'm not going to be able to finish so-and-so in time." When dealing with people who are at this stage, it's a good idea to begin discussions with an evaluation of what the most important goal is and look at all the options that will get us from point A to point B in the time frame we require. When we're in this mindset, we may need help identifying the alternatives available to us.

Mindset #4: Acceptance

Finally convinced that a new way is necessary, we admit that we have a lot to learn and start from scratch. At least we're attempting to develop new abilities! Typically, in this mindset, we ask for help: "Can you show me how you . . . ?" Obviously, the best strategy here for managers is to make sure the person gets the help he or she needs. When we're in this mindset, and not before, we're ready to try out new ways of doing things.

Mindset #5: Testing New Behaviors

We explore the limits of the skills we are now actively developing. Typically, in this mindset, we say things like, "I think I'm getting the hang of it." At this point, managers and trainers should celebrate any success—no matter how small—and minimize the long-term importance of any failure. When we're in this mindset, we're hungry for reinforcement!

Mindset #6: New Applications

We start to apply the newly acquired skills to new situations; we start to ask unique questions based on our own experience and capabilities. Typically, in this mindset, we ask questions like, "What if I do thus-and-so?" or "Could I use this same idea in a different way by changing such-and-such?" This is where managers and trainers need to support brainstorming sessions on either the small or large scales and also need to make sure great new ideas get recorded, reviewed, and implemented!

CHAPTER 27

Tales of a Cable Installer

If you don't know where you are going, you might wind up someplace else.

—YOGI BERRA

- ♦ What does the upselling conversation look like one-on-one?
- ♦ How is it navigated?
- ♦ What role do questions about the other person's world play in the upselling discussion?

ABOUT A YEAR AND A HALF AGO, a cable installer came by to fix your cable box.

"By the way," he said, pulling stuff out of his toolbox, "do you have any kids?"

You said that you did.

"How many?"

You told him that you had two boys and a girl.

"What kind of stuff do they watch?"

You explain that they liked cartoons.

"Well that's interesting," he said. "Did you ever think of . . ."

At this point he reeled off half a dozen possible channels that were in a premium service package that he offered.

You had to admit it sounded very interesting.

"By the way, you like boxing?"

You said you didn't like boxing, but you were a golf fan. You had a long talk about golf, and while he was fixing the cable box, you each shared stories about triumphs and tragedies on the green.

"Did you know they have a special channel devoted just to golf now?"

"No, I didn't know that," you answered.

You share a pleasant conversation. At the end of twenty minutes, during which time he was supposedly only fixing your cable box, he had learned enough about your family—and you about his—for the two of you to consider each other something more than acquaintances, but something less than close friends. Business acquaintances, if you will.

All of a sudden, he was your cable consultant.

"Well," he says, putting stuff back in his toolbox, "I'll tell you what I would do if I were you. I'd take a look at . . ."

And at this point, he shows you a brochure for three premium-channel packages.

Before he leaves, you've signed up for all three.

CHAPTER 28

The Simplest Upselling Strategy of Them All

Things should be as simple as possible, but not simpler.
—ALBERT EINSTEIN

- ♦ What about upselling letters?
- ♦ What should they look like?
- ♦ Whom should they go to?
- ♦ How much time should we spend on them?

WHEN WE TALK ABOUT UPSELLING, it is tempting to think of the process as requiring some—or even a great deal—of our time as salespeople each week. But what if you were able to make a very tiny investment of time up front, an investment that would pay off and deliver additional sales to you and your organization for weeks, months, and even years and years to come?

That is exactly what you can do by developing an upselling letter. Actually, I prefer to think of this letter as a modified thank-you letter, because it really serves as an excuse to upsell though its formal purpose is simply to thank the person for his or her business.

This letter will take you—or someone in your organization who is good at writing this kind of thing—no more than an hour to put together. But it will deliver astonishing results to you in terms of expanded sales from your customers and clients.

Here's what it looks like:

Dear (name):

Thank you so much for your recent order. We appreciate your choice to do business with our company and know that you have a choice when it comes to purchasing sales training.

I will be acting as your personal contact for the upcoming program. It is now scheduled to take place on January 5, (year). The topic of the program, as we discussed, is "Getting in the Door."

I know it will be of great value to your sales team.

If you need to contact me for any reason between now and the scheduled date of the program, I hope you will reach out to me using any of the numbers below:

My business number: (212) 555-1212
My personal cell phone: (212) 555-1213
My number at home, where I can be reached after 7:00 P.M.: (212) 555-6868

You can also reach me by means of my e-mail address, which is joesmith@deisales.com.

By the way, (name), you may be interested to learn that we are also offering a special this month on our e-learning programs. These are self-teaching diagnostic tools that your salespeople can use to sharpen their selling skills after the training. You can find an overview of the e-learning programs we offer as reinforcement to the main program at www.dei-sales.com. If you are interested in exploring this option for your sales team, please feel free to contact me at any of the numbers above.

Thanks again for choosing D.E.I. Management Group,
Mike Ryan
D.E.I. Management Group

You see how it works? The point is to send out a thank-you letter that identifies you or someone in your organization as a critical touch point following the order. *In the same communication,* you will casually mention whatever special you or your organization is offering that month and encourage the contact to reach out to the touch-point person for further information on ordering it. You can change the offer month by month, expand it, or even revise the entire letter. But my advice is that for people who purchase from you for the first time, you always send out some kind of letter that follows the general outline of what you see above. It is a time investment of such minimal scope that you may not even notice how long it takes. But if you make a practice of sending this out to each new customer, you will certainly notice the inquiries that come your way from people who have just decided to buy from you.

CHAPTER 29

When You Work for a Large Organization

The best executive is the one who has sense enough to pick good men to do what he wants done, and self-restraint to keep from meddling with them while they do it.

—THEODORE ROOSEVELT

- ◆ What initiatives are especially important to our upselling efforts if we work for a large company or organization?
- ◆ What can go wrong?
- ◆ What resources can we bring to our customer's side?
- ◆ What kind of face-to-face interactions should we encourage?

THE FOLLOWING IMPORTANT UPSELLING RULES will be of interest to people who work in companies that sometimes present bureaucratic obstacles to their customers. You really can solidify your relationship and improve your upselling chances by adopting each of these principles. My general rule of thumb is that, if the prospect or customer calling you cannot reach you directly within one hour, you need to implement *all* of these ideas.

Principle #1: *Make Sure You Are Reachable*

No ifs, ands, or buts. If that means investing in your own cell phone or BlackBerry unit and paying for that out of your own pocket, then do so. Your customers must be able to reach you no matter what. If they have difficulty doing so, you will lose out to the competition.

Principle #2: *Share the Easter Eggs*

You know what Easter eggs are. They are the secret parts of DVDs that you find out about only after somebody who really knows all the ins and outs of the fan club newsletter shares them with you. So, let's say you are looking at the DVD for *Citizen Kane*. You might have the DVD around for six months or a year before you realize there is a special feature that is not on the main menu—something that you have to access by positioning the cursor on a graphic that did not look like it was part of the formal user interface. Well, if you know somebody who is a big *Citizen Kane* fan, he can point you toward all the Easter eggs on the DVD and show you how to get to the cool stuff quickly without waiting six months or stumbling across it on your own. The same principle applies to your own customers. You should make a point of listing things that are of added value that you can deliver for your customers—all the things that nobody else within the organization is likely to tell them. It might be a Web site that has the answers to critical questions. It might be a special toolkit or premium that your president has authorized for distribution to a select few key accounts. It might even be your own expertise in resolving typical challenges and opportunities that your customers face—a Frequently Asked Questions page of your own, if you will. Whatever it is, come up with at least three things that you can help your customers access within your organization. Make sure each and every one of your customers, at least the ones you want to hold on to, receives your "Easter eggs."

Principle #3: *Introduce the Family*

Do not just dash off to the Caribbean for three weeks and leave your customers high and dry. Pick someone you trust to handle their inevitable questions, crises, and suggestions. Schedule a conference call or even a face-to-face meeting to introduce the person who will be covering for you in your absence.

Principle #4: *Build Your Own Company*

It sounds crazy, but it really is how things get done in big organizations. There are subcompanies that emerge within larger companies. These are not formal business entities, of course, but they are loosely or not-so-loosely arranged alliances and communication networks. If you do not know who the four most important people you work with in your organization are, you should—and your clients should, too. Identify your own mini organization chart and share it with your key contacts.

Principle #5: *Get Them a Meeting with Your President*

If you cannot arrange a meeting with the company president, then get the highest-ranking person you can find. Look the person in the eye. Say, "It will help me hold on to this account if you spend half an hour with me today at lunch." If that person turns you down for whatever reason, work your way around your own organization and find someone else.

Principle #6: *Give Them a Tour*

Salespeople are very big on touring the facilities of our prospects, but it probably is just as important that your most important customers see how your operation runs, too. Anyone who is critical to your sales success should have a clear sense of how your company operates, and that means firsthand experience. This is one situation where face-to-face really does make a difference. The bigger the account, the more trouble you should go to to try to arrange for face-to-face interaction.

Principle #7: *Send a Book*

Whatever book you happen to be reading, if you think it is of interest to your prospects and customers, find a reason to send a copy inscribed with your own signature. Of course, if the book represents your company in some way—the autobiography of your CEO, let's say—that is all the better. But if this is not possible, and often it is not, just be sure to humanize your contact's relationship with your company by sending along a book that you have read and think the prospect will find interesting and valuable. One piece of advice: Keep it business related.

CHAPTER 30

"Just Focus on Him"

Someone sent me a postcard picture of the earth. On the back it said, "Wish you were here."

—STEPHEN WRIGHT

- ♦ How important is personal attention to the upselling process?
- ♦ Why can't we expect to make upselling relationships work by focusing on ourselves?
- ♦ Just what does Tom Hanks have to do with all this?

THERE IS A SCENE IN THE MOVIE *SLEEPLESS IN SEATTLE*, at the top of the Empire State Building, in which Meg Ryan is standing and staring at her costar, Tom Hanks. This scene took quite a long time to shoot. The director had to stop several times and ask Ryan to simplify her performance. Apparently, the first few takes were fascinating and filled with activity, but they were not exactly what the director was looking for. Finally, in an effort to make sure that the all-important scene atop the Empire State Building came off correctly, the director gave Meg Ryan a very simple piece of advice: "It's really all about him. Just focus on him."

That simple piece of acting advice utterly changed the dynamics of the scene—and the entire film. By reminding Meg Ryan that the point of the scene was to focus with 100 percent attention on her costar, the director managed to capture that most appealing of all human decisions, namely, the decision to focus all of one's resources and listening power and experiences on another human being.

That is what made the movie work, as it turned out. That is what makes romance work. And that is, I submit, what ultimately makes upselling campaigns work.

I shared with you earlier a few thoughts on the importance of moving from the initial "vendor" stages of a relationship up to the "resource" stage of the relationship and becoming a trusted business ally and a strategic partner in the process. I really do not think that it is possible for any salesperson to do that unless you are willing to focus on your prospect or customer with the same kind of relaxed, focused, accepting attention that Meg Ryan showed in that critical scene in *Sleepless in Seattle*. (Go ahead—check out the movie sometime and take a look. And while you are watching it, notice the factual error when Meg Ryan dashes into the Empire State Building and pleads to be let onto the observation deck. How she gets through without having to wait in line for a ticket or how she manages to skirt the line to the elevator are beyond me—but hey, these are the movies, and I am just a New Yorker who knows how things really work.)

In real life, we cannot expect to make our relationships work by focusing on ourselves. That is true as we enter our marriage, and it is true as we enter any business relationship. The simplest and easiest prescription for succeeding in the all-important task of moving to the top of the pyramid is to spend as much time, energy, and attention on the other person as possible and to make it a holy mission to fulfill that person's objectives—within the guidelines of your own ethical and business capacities, of course.

CHAPTER 31

Pull Out Your Legal Pad

He who would learn to fly one day must first learn to stand and walk and run and climb and dance; one cannot fly into flying.

—FRIEDRICH NIETZSCHE

♦ Why is note taking—the old-fashioned way—critical early in building rapport with our customers?
♦ What advantages does it bring to the discussion?
♦ How does it pave the way for a richer conversation and bring about a better upselling environment?

HERE'S ONE OF MY FAVORITE STRATEGIES for moving toward "strategic partner" status: start small and gather one fact at a time—with old-fashioned pen-and-pad technology.

We live in a high-tech world, and sometimes I think that that technology does not always serve us with perfect efficiency. Let me share with you what I mean. Most of the salespeople whom I train will begin a meeting with a prospect by saying, "Let me show you a PowerPoint that we put together for the people we want to do work with."

At that point, they begin paging through a generic PowerPoint that is designed specifically for nobody and generically for everybody. This is basically a twenty-first-century equivalent of the common problem of "throwing up" all over the prospect by reading verbatim from the brochure, only it feels a little bit less like that because the person uses the PowerPoint as a tool to hold what could be mistaken for a conversation with the other person.

To my way of thinking, this is a huge mistake and a violation of the rule that I have just shared with you here for success in upselling, namely, that we must be sure to focus every conceivable atom of our attention on the other person during our meetings. This point is particularly important in the first meeting, but it applies to all subsequent meetings as well.

Consider the advantages of the old-fashioned legal-pad-and-pen approach.

- By pulling out the legal pad and your pen, without asking for permission to do so, you make a subtle but important point. You are here in a professional capacity and you are here to do a job. That job is to take down information from this person or group of people.
- By maintaining eye contact with the key people in the room, nodding briskly, and then jotting down key points on the legal pad, you will be sending the message that you take seriously every piece of information the prospect is giving you.
- By having your legal pad out during the meeting, you can use it to develop impromptu sketches and diagrams and adapt as necessary when you receive corrections from the people you are talking to.
- By taking the time and trouble to actually write down notes by hand, you will be demonstrating that you are willing to do more than most salespeople do—and indeed more than most people in any field of endeavor do—and will be willing to make a personal commitment to get things right, even if it takes a little bit more time and effort.
- At the end of the meeting, you can review all of the key points that you have taken down by hand and begin a recap of all of the essential information from the meeting, one that begins with a phrase similar to "Well, here's what I got from you so far. . . ."

I am not saying that you should never use a PowerPoint presentation in your conversations with prospects and customers. What I am saying is that, if you do use one, what you must do—at least if you want to move forward into the "resource" phase of the relationship that I am emphasizing in this book—is build a *customized* PowerPoint deck that is based on the notes you take by hand. In all likelihood, you should save that for the second substantial meeting with the committee or person to whom you are trying to upsell.

These days, of course, the first meeting may well take place by means of a conference call or other remote meeting format. In this case, your best bet will be to reach out by phone *before the meeting,* and do your note taking by hand then! Yes, you certainly can take notes over the phone, and you get most if not all of the benefits of doing so in person simply by mentioning to your contact that you are doing so. You can pull this off by using phrases like the following at key points in the conversation:

- "Hold on, let me get my pad out—I want to take some notes."
- "Let me be sure I've got this correct in my notes—what you're saying is . . ."
- "So let me just recap what I've heard so far—this is what I've got down in my notes . . ."

CHAPTER 32

What's the Next Step?

When the solution is simple, God is answering.
                                        —ALBERT EINSTEIN

- ♦ What is a Next Step?
- ♦ Why is it so important?
- ♦ How do I get one?
- ♦ What does it mean if a customer won't give me one?

I BELIEVE ALL EFFECTIVE UPSELLING is based on developing urgency in the relationship. If someone isn't willing to make a time commitment to speak with you, meet with you, or put you in touch with other people, that's not a good sign. One of my cardinal selling rules is that we always want to get the other person to do something. Ideally, we want the other person to do something that results in measurable action that is scheduled for the short term.

That's a little bit of a cumbersome phrase, "measurable action that is scheduled for the short term," so I use a shorthand version: Next Step.

A Next Step is something someone puts in his or her calendar that shows a willingness to meet, discuss, or otherwise interact with you at some point between now and two weeks from now.

What's so special about two weeks from now? Well, one of the things we've noticed over the years in our company is that there are two very different types of time commitments. There is the kind of time commitment where I say to you that I'm willing to meet with you at some point, and then there's the time commitment where I say to you that I'm willing to meet with you at a point in time specifically between now and the next two weeks.

What's interesting is that even if I get specific and offer you a time slot that is for more than two weeks from now, let's say, the day after New Year's, and it's October, that commitment has a statistical likelihood to go unfulfilled. It starts to drop right after the two-week mark. And it's easy to see why. We live our lives in two-week chunks. If you talk to the average business person and get a look at his or her calendar, what you'll find is that there's a great deal of specific information about what's happening on the calendar between now and the end of the period that's two weeks from now. You'll find much less specificity and much less competition for slots two weeks further and out. This is not a hard-and-fast rule, but it is a general guideline.

So think about the implications of this. The part of the schedule that we're focusing on is, inevitably, that which is on our horizon: whatever is happening within the next two weeks. The part of our schedule that we're not focusing on is the part that is two weeks or more ahead. What this means is that someone who is trying to put you off—but who really doesn't want to say, "I have no intention of meeting with you or discussing this with you"—can do so simply by saying, "Let's schedule it for four weeks from now."

It's even possible that someone who genuinely means to get together with us or speak with us or have a conference call with us, and simply is booked between now and two weeks from now, will innocently place us in the schedule for four or five or six weeks from now, simply because that's when most slots are available. But guess what? When the person finally gets that week into the two-week "horizon" of real-world commitments, there will be other priorities! Something that was important enough not to move six weeks out will find its way into that person's schedule, and we'll be bumped again or perhaps even forgotten about.

This phenomenon is familiar to virtually every salesperson on the face of the earth who's worthy of the name. If you've ever set a meeting with someone for four weeks ahead of time and then failed to confirm that the meeting was taking place and simply showed up on the person's doorstep at the appointed time, you have no doubt had the experience of having your meeting supplanted by some other, suddenly more important, activity.

So when we say that a Next Step must take place at some point within the next two weeks, what we're really saying is that we're asking the people to whom we're trying to upsell to make a clear assessment to us of exactly how important this discussion or meeting or conference call really is to them. That's not how we say it, of course, but it's how we can measure it. If the person is willing to set aside a specific chunk of time within that critical time frame that embraces the next two weeks, then we can rest assured that we are dealing with someone who's really interested in talking to us. If, on the other hand, the person puts us off time and time again or "schedules" time to talk with us that is a month or more down the line, we can make a realistic assessment that this person really isn't all that interested in interacting with us. That's not to say he or she couldn't be interested in interacting with us at some point, but it is helpful to us in prioritizing where we're putting our time, effort, and energy to know who's a true upselling prospect.

| CHAPTER 33 |

"Based on What We've Discussed Today . . ."

Leadership is the art of getting someone else to do something you want done because he wants to do it.
—Dwight Eisenhower

♦ How can I use this phase to help generate Next Steps?
♦ What kind of Next Steps should I be asking for?
♦ What does the Next Step I schedule with my customer tell me about the quality of my relationship with that customer?

Here's another set of upselling "magic words": *"Based on what we've discussed today . . ."* Okay, maybe they're not really *magic*. But they can be quite powerful. Take a look:

• "Based on what we've discussed today, I want to come back here on February fourth at ten o'clock and show you some ideas of how we might be able to work together on this new project. Before we get together, would you be able to . . ."
• "Based on what we've discussed today, I'm excited about what we're talking about—but I'll be honest, I'm a little concerned about (the price/the timing/your budget/whatever). What's your feeling on that?"
• "Based on what we've discussed today, let me ask you something—just between you and me, what do you think is really going to happen here?"

- "If I came in and met all your criteria next week, could you see us doing business together again?"
  ("Well, it all depends on Mel, because Mel makes all those decisions with me. . . .")
- "You know what? I'm thinking it makes sense for you and I and Mel to get together. Based on what we've talked about here today, does that make sense to you?"

When you have a Next Step, you have something. When you don't have a Next Step, you've got nothing. Among the reasons you can offer for getting together with someone are the following:

- A chance to strategize before a committee meeting
- A chance to debrief after a committee meeting (I am a big fan of setting these postcommittee sessions *before* the actual meeting takes place with my contact.)
- A tour of the facility
- A chance to meet the president of your company
- A chance to meet the president of the prospect's company
- A chance to meet with the prospect's team
- A chance to report back on what you think the prospect's team is doing right
- A chance to report back on what you think the prospect's team is doing wrong
- A chance to explain how you think you can implement the prospect's plan for the next month, quarter, or year
- A chance to explain why you think the prospect's plan for the next month, quarter, or year will not work.
- A chance for the prospect to see your product or service in action.
- A chance for the prospect to see *you* in action. (This is particularly effective if you are a trainer, technical expert, salesperson, or on-site consultant. If there is something you do and do well, feel free to invite the prospect to watch you do it, especially if there is any showmanship you can incorporate at some point in the proceedings.)
- A chance to see a product demonstration.

- A chance to visit or have a conference call with a happy customer of yours.
- A highly customized PowerPoint presentation delivered in person.
- A highly customized PowerPoint presentation delivered online.

Just be sure that you're taking plenty of notes and not missing the key points. And watch out for body language to make sure that the person is not drifting off.

This is just a few of the many, many, many things you can do to develop some sort of Next Step with the person you hope to sell more of your product or service to. It has been my experience that all that is really necessary, if there is a meaningful relationship in place already, and sometimes even if there is not, is for you to call your contact up and say, "Hey listen, I have an idea that I want to discuss with you, and I think we should get together in person to do it."

That is perhaps the most powerful test of whether or not you have a real relationship going. If you do not, and if your prospect is not willing to make that investment of time and effort with you to discuss your idea, then perhaps you should try to reach out to somebody else in the organization.

CHAPTER 34

Meet Billy Mitchell

I don't measure a man's success by how high he climbs but how high he bounces when he hits bottom.
—GENERAL GEORGE S. PATTON

♦ Who was Billy Mitchell?
♦ What does he have to do with upselling to the larger organization?
♦ What did he do that I should model in my own upselling initiatives?
♦ What mistakes did he make that I should avoid?

LET'S LOOK AT THE TASK of upselling as it plays out when your customer is a large organization.

This is certainly one of the most challenging areas of all for the inexperienced salesperson—and even for the experienced one. In fact, the job of getting larger and larger amounts of business from very large accounts (and their accompanying bureaucracies) is one of the more challenging tasks for any sales department. A good number of companies, in recent years, have opted for the strategy of simply splitting the company's sales efforts in two: in other words, devoting half of the sales staff to the task of developing new business, and half of the sales staff to the task of maintaining, and hopefully expanding, one's presence in major accounts that the company controls.

The goal is to win business—and larger orders—over time from companies where decision making is spread out over a broad organizational structure. In order to get our bearings with this topic,

I want to ask you to take a look at the life story of a man who exemplifies the kind of strategy and dedication required to convince a large bureaucracy to change its ways and do something a little bit differently—and more productively. His name is Billy Mitchell.

William L. (Billy) Mitchell is regarded today as the father of the United States Air Force. Just as John Adams, in his day, saw a yawning chasm of disaster awaiting the United States if it did not speedily develop a navy, Mitchell saw correctly, as early as 1905, that the most strategically important combat operations of the future would take place not on the ground, but in the air.

He was born in France in 1879; his father was a rich man and a senator from the state of Wisconsin. When he was eighteen years old, he signed up for duty as a private during the Spanish-American War. Not long after that, he joined the Army Signal Corps and later served in the Philippines and in Alaska. At the tender age of thirty-two, he was appointed to the army's general staff. It was around this period that he became interested in aviation. He paid for his own flying lessons at the age of thirty-eight. He had to, because the army believed that thirty-eight was too old for an aspiring pilot. Besides, at that point he was regarded as too high up in the command chain to be assigned to flight training.

Mitchell showed up in France shortly after the American entry into World War I. At this point, he was lieutenant colonel with some aviation experience, which made him an important figure in the theater of war. Having quickly established the choices and objectives of his French and British counterparts and having more or less devoured whole the history of the air war up to that point, Mitchell assumed responsibility for the air effort of the American side. Before the war was out, he had developed a flashy image as an inexhaustible commander, won the rank of brigadier general, and assumed responsibility for all U.S. combat troops in France. In September 1918, the Battle of Saint-Mihiel gave him the opportunity to display his leadership abilities while commanding airborne units. It was the first air campaign in American history, and Mitchell was at the head of it.

In the years after the war, Mitchell repeatedly criticized the strategy and preparedness of the U.S. military, and in 1925, he was brought up on charges of insubordination. After a court-martial, Mitchell resigned his commission in 1926. That same year, the air service with which he had been so strongly associated was transformed into the U.S. Army Air Corps, and over the next decade—with him off the scene—a ramping up of American airpower began. In 1941, five years after Mitchell's death, the Army Air Corps evolved into the U.S. Army Air Force, and in 1943, it achieved separate status coequal with that of the army and the navy. Far from being a restless malcontent whose only goal was self-aggrandizement, Mitchell was eventually recognized as the farsighted, if controversial, military thinker who had seen and spotlighted enormous gaps in the American defense system. The B-25 bombers used against Japan in 1942, a retaliation for the attacks on Pearl Harbor, which he had so accurately predicted, were named after Billy Mitchell. Mitchell was the recipient of a posthumous medal celebrating his contributions to military aviation in 1946; the air force, which owed its existence to his vision, formally rendered null and void Mitchell's court-martial in 1955. In 1957, the air force responded to family efforts to clear Mitchell's name by issuing a statement of regret about the grim conclusion of Mitchell's military career.

The point I want to make about upselling to large organizations is not that you should follow Mitchell's example and step on as many toes as possible, not that you should seek public recognition for your ideas, and not that you should be ready and willing to alienate important people. Instead, the lesson I want you to take from Mitchell's story is that there are times when one is justified in taking a stand—even when that stand goes against one's perceived own interests.

Mitchell knew that he was right about the importance of the development of American airpower, and he also knew that the military establishment was unlikely to make the investments necessary to bring about the needed changes. There was turf to be protected, there were careers to be protected, and there were precedents to be maintained. But Mitchell knew that the system needed to change, and so he set about changing it, even at the expense of his own career.

Please understand that I am not saying you can or should risk your job or your career while you attempt to upsell to a major account. What you should be aware of, though, is that major accounts are slow to change and that one person on a mission within the account may be more powerful than thirty people carrying out ideas that worked forty years ago. If you were to take Mitchell's willingness to look around corners, his vision, and his commitment and combine them with a willingness to form alliances and build consensus, you would have my ideal model for upselling in the major account environment. The trick is, as we have seen elsewhere, to be more concerned about what you see on the horizon than the prospect is.

There are definitely lessons to be learned from the experience of Billy Mitchell. We know from his experience that bureaucracies can be very difficult to tame. Getting anyone to change anything in a hierarchy, especially a large hierarchy, can be quite challenging. There is a famous story about AT&T that is worth remembering in this regard. An AT&T employee once observed that the company was a little like an oversized dragon. You could kick it in the tail as hard as you wanted, but it wouldn't feel it for the next year and a half. Then, after those eighteen months had elapsed, you'd hear the dragon say ouch.

The person who passed along this anecdote was none other than the chairman of AT&T!

So, these are experiences and insights about large organizations that Billy Mitchell, if anyone, learned firsthand. They sometimes require change, they are resistant to change, and they're sometimes openly hostile to it.

Let's look at the ways Billy Mitchell *did not* further his cause and see what we can learn from them.

From all accounts, when he had unpleasant truths to tell, he told them without assembling any consensus or constituency that would help translate them into meaningful change. This is, perhaps, the difference between a prophet in the Old Testament and a states-man doing his duties for a company, organization, or country in dire need of reform. It is difficult to imagine anyone reforming the mili-tary—or indeed any large-scale organization—without developing an understanding for the egos, eccentricities, and sometimes childish prejudices of those deeply human beings who inhabit it. The same principle, I'm afraid, holds true for major accounts. It is perhaps a little better and a little wiser to choose the statesman model rather than play the role of the prophet of doom.

In dealing with large accounts, don't place too much signifi-cance on being right. Take a look at your constituencies and at your own communication style. Think of Billy Mitchell. Do emulate his foresight, his ability to take practical experience and apply it to the future of the organization about which he cared so dearly, and his willingness to put his own career and interests on the line. Think twice, however, before you adopt his intransigence, his unwillingness to change, and his inability to build meaningful coalitions based on the interests of the parties with whom he was dealing.

If there is one thing Billy Mitchell failed to do during his remarkable career, it was make someone else look good. And that, as it turns out, is an essential skill for upselling within the large account, as you'll learn in the next chapter.

CHAPTER 35

The Art of Making People Look Good

A leader is a dealer in hope.
—Napoleon Bonaparte

♦ What is the company trying to get accomplished?
♦ What is the individual trying to get accomplished within the company?
♦ Why is making somebody else look good such an important upselling skill?
♦ How do you do it?

Companies are constantly changing. Not only our own company, of course, but the company we're trying to sell to, as well. *But . . .* not every single person in every company knows every change that is coming.

Generally, the higher up I sell my products and services, the more likely I am to find the one person who's familiar with all the changes on the horizon. However, there is a challenge. It's not enough for me just to spend time with a key decision maker; I have to add value, and I have to know how to make the person look good within his or her organization.

Don't confuse the quantity of time with the quality of the relationship. Just because you play golf with a person, that does not mean you have a partnership or a resource relationship going. If you are in a resource relationship, you have instant access to anybody within the company if you want it. If you are in a resource relationship, you can ask, "How come you are doing it that way?" and you will get a meaningful answer. If you have a resource relationship, you could ask the person who is buying your stuff, "How are you prepared to handle such and such a problem?" And the person would say to you, "We were coming to you guys tomorrow morning to ask about that. How do you think that we should handle it?"

You will know that you are not at the top of the relationship pyramid if the problem is one that you can solve, yet the customer does not call you first. In that case, you are lower down on the pyramid, and the question you should be asking is, "How come you are talking to them?"

For example, I could go to the CEO of a company that's already buying training from us and ask what changes are happening in his telesales department. He would probably have an overview of the kinds of missions that they're on. But he's not necessarily going to know what kind of software they're going to use.

So, my goal is to position my upsell properly—and the key to positioning the upsell is, on the most basic level, to find something that is going to help someone do what they're trying to do and look great in the process. That's the part of the equation that Billy Mitchell missed.

But what are they trying to do? That's the $64,000 question.

For most companies, it breaks down this way: What they're trying to do is . . .

- Gain market share
- Gain a competitive edge in the marketplace
- Improve/increase revenues
- Increase/improve profits

Those are the big four from the company's point of view. So, in order to do that, of course, companies do all kinds of things. They improve sales, improve the people, recruit better people, and try to retain better people. They try to improve their customer service, reduce attrition, and increase retention (which improves the profit per sale and reduces the cost of sale). They try to make their companies more attractive to investors by becoming more productive, more efficient, and less wasteful or by increasing their profit margin. Those are the ways companies carry out those four big goals. Basically, they're trying to make more money, keep more money, and position themselves right for the future.

But what companies do isn't the whole picture. What do *individuals* in the company try to do?

Well, typically, they're trying to change things in their own lives. Specifically, they're trying to . . .

- Get a raise and/or a promotion
- Change the amount of work they do
- Change the amount of perceived power and status they have
- Change the actual level of control they have over specific events in their department

So, with the individual—and ultimately, I believe, it always does come down to individuals—the goal is to make the person you're working with *look so good* that he or she makes progress toward one or more of these goals.

Help them look good in order to get a raise and a promotion. Help them look good in order to change their perceived power and status. And so forth. Do that through the person's own department/division, which is helping the company achieve its goals.

For example, this morning I had breakfast with the president and head of a major media company that had already purchased training from us for his field salespeople. My goal is to sell him training for his telesales group as well—a classic upselling situation, from my point of view. He bought A, and it worked out well for him. Now I think he should buy B.

He doesn't know (for instance) what specific kind of phone system they have, but he did tell me that what they're looking to do on an overall level is to improve every department—in fact, he told me, there's a department heads meeting going on right now. And they're all looking at getting more sales out of every department.

I said, "What's going on with your telesales department?"

He said, "Well, we're trying to get more sales out of that group."

I said, "Okay, why are you looking to get more sales out of telesales?"

He said, "Well, you know, we're just trying to get more sales out of everybody."

"Listen," I said. "Let me just tell you something. Companies that I know that improve their telesales and that also have a field sales group find that every dollar they can get out of telesales has a lower cost per sale. Every sale made by the telesales group is a sale that the field salespeople, who are more expensive, don't have to make. So, the higher level of sale you're able to accomplish on the phone, the more profitable sales are left for the more expensive salespeople. If you find the right balance, you could actually increase sales slightly through telesales and dramatically improve your margins."

What does that help him do? Look like a hero to the board of directors. This is obviously the kind of relationship we want to have. And notice that I put it into language that he can understand: improving margins.

If you stop and think about it, people are motivated by the desire to look good in front of other people. It is just human nature. They are also motivated by the fear of looking bad in front of other people. These are really two sides of the same coin. However you approach it, any upselling initiative that reduces the likelihood that somebody is going to look like an idiot, or that increases the likelihood that somebody is going to look like a hero, is likely to help you build bridges and turn a onetime customer into a repeat customer.

The truth of the matter is, though, that you really cannot do this unless you have expertise or value that you yourself can add in a unique way as a representative of your company. Take a look again at what I was able to do with that CEO of that media company. I found the area where I knew a little bit more than he did—okay, maybe more than a little bit more—and I made a direct appeal to something that was true in my experience, namely, that telesales departments are there for a very valid budgetary reason. They are cheaper than field sales departments. This is not to say that field sales departments are unnecessary, but it is to say that in many situations, it makes just as much sense financially to train your telesales people to operate at peak efficiency as it does to train your field sales people to operate at peak efficiency. In fact, it makes far more sense!

So, this is a piece of value that I was able to deliver to him, and it ended up making him look great in front of his audience, his board of directors. As a result, we have gotten quite a lot of business from this company. Now the example I have given you sounds very high-end and very complex and very corporate, but I can tell you that the same precise relationship is in play every time you reach out to another human being and share some piece of value that you have about how what you offer impacts how good they are going to look in front of somebody else. Specifically, if you are selling exercise equipment, you do not go and spend your whole afternoon harping about how wonderful the equipment is because it has this feature and that electrical attachment and this conversion ratio. Instead, you want to share real-life stories or, better yet, your own real-life experience with using the equipment. How much weight did you lose? How much weight did somebody that you know lose? How did it affect your social life? How did it affect the way you were perceived at work?

Notice that precisely the same model is at work in the high-end sale—looking great in front of a board of directors because you have been able to reduce the cost of sales—and the low-end upsell—looking great because you have lost fifteen pounds in fifteen days. The point is, if you are credible, if you are enthusiastic, and if you are committed to making the other person look good, you really can get the other person interested not only in what you are offering this time around as an upsell, but also in all the other materials that you may be able to pass along over the next weeks and months and even years.

Well, let's return to my example. Suppose I had to approach the guy who's in charge of telesales and try to win new training business from him rather than from the CEO. He's in charge of telesales and is trying to look good to his company so that he can get a raise and promotion. But I can't take the same approach with him that I would with the CEO.

What I could do with him is to say, "Listen, what I could help you guys do is this. Right now, you can't increase talk time, you can't increase the lead base, you can't increase the head count. But what I can do is help you to reduce the amount of wasted time your people spend on the phone. That will decrease your queue times, improve your customer retention, reduce attrition, and improve customer satisfaction. Basically, I can help you drive your numbers up. And I can show your people how to make an upselling presentation that will enable them to increase the average value of the call they close over the phone. And I can show you how to measure all that, and guess what? You're going to look like a hero when you have the numbers to show off to your CEO."

Managers must be given ammunition to prove that they are good managers. In this case, if I were approaching a manager to get him to buy into the idea of expanding my company's relationship with his, I am going to have to do so not by pointing out that his salespeople are paid less than other salespeople in the organization, but rather by giving him access to tools that will help him to generate a spreadsheet that proves what a great job he is doing with the resources he has. It is a different rhetorical emphasis, and it is a different piece of strategy.

When you are dealing with managers on the front lines, people whose job it is to deliver the results and keep the teams pointed in the right direction, think of the tasks they face in a world dominated by the obsession of cutting costs and trimming away "fat." This person is interested, first and foremost, in proving to the rest of the company that he and his people do not equate to "fat" in any way, shape, or form. So, as you approach these decision makers and advocates in the upselling process, remember that their take on what will turn them into a hero usually depends on your ability to prove that they are not only doing a job, but doing it well and nobly.

Now, suppose my job were to go to the telesales people and turn *them* into allies for the idea of purchasing another training program from my company, a program designed specifically for them. Here's what I would say to them: "Now, what you guys want to do is, you want to make more money, am I right? So here's how you make more money. You want to increase the average value of your call, and here's how you do that, by building this 'by the way' step into your closing process."

Notice that I'm talking about the same component of the training but *identifying a different benefit*. Here, when I'm appealing to the actual salespeople, my goal is to focus on increasing personal income. I have to keep repositioning my upselling effort to match the audience I've targeted.

CHAPTER 36

The Follow-Through Campaign

The leadership instinct you are born with is the backbone.
You develop the funny bone and the wishbone that go with it.
                                                    —ELAINE AGATHER

- ♦ Why are follow-through campaigns so important to our upselling efforts?
- ♦ How should we introduce them?
- ♦ How can we use them to sell more?

IN MY COMPANY, which is a sales training company, we have a pretty simple strategy for developing new business from our existing clients. We tell them exactly what we want to do next.

Actually, as a precursor to that, what we do is, we take the radical step of being very honest with them very early on in the relationship.

When I am meeting with a decision maker who is considering purchasing things from our company, I will say something like the following to him: "I am going to tell you the secret of the sales training industry, a secret that most people do not want to share with you, but that we tell each and every person that we work with. Sales training does not work—unless you reinforce it. If you simply do two days of training this month and then never do anything else, what you have is a motivational event and results will trail off, even if the people you are training get some real benefit from the things that they have been taught. However, if you do the program, you pass along the information, you give people the strategies they can really use, and you follow up a month afterward with a conference call and a face-to-face refresher session, then your results are going to be dramatically better. You are going to be able to sustain the improvement, and you will be in a much better position to build it into the way that people operate day after day after day. If you just rely on sales training, it does not work—because it does not permanently affect behavior. If, on the other hand, you rely on sales training and effective reinforcement, you can change people's habits and change the culture of the organization. And that is what we always recommend our clients do."

Now, every word of what I have just shared with you about what I said about clients is true. Strategically, it really does make the most possible sense to build policy programs into every sales-training event. But just as there is no effective training program without a follow-through, there is also (in my experience) no meaningful upselling strategy in our industry without a follow-through.

We have a number of training programs that we offer, but typically the people we work with come in looking to fix only one thing. So, they come to us for help in, for instance, setting more new first appointments. That is the main item on the agenda. We know it, they know it, and it is the only thing they want to focus on right at the outset of the relationship.

Well, as it happens, we can do both the training program and the reinforcement program that will permanently change the way an organization develops new leads and makes first appointments. However, we offer a lot more than that, too. So, what we will do, in the ideal situation, is establish both the training program and the reinforcement program for that initial appointment-making piece, and then during the reinforcement piece, the follow-through piece, the checkup piece, we will develop a strategy for sharing the *other* training programs that we have to offer with our prospects and customers.

When there is a reinforcement session to do the diagnostic work, that diagnostic session will allow us to point out where else we can add value. That is how we take a client who may otherwise be thinking about a single program and extend that relationship into four or five or six or more programs over time.

The key to making this work is simple: The diagnoses we make are valid!

The teams who have learned how to set first appointments *really should* move on to the next programs in the sequence, and their overall numbers *really do* go up as a result of doing so! But they would never have gotten the chance to improve in that way if we had not scheduled the posttraining meetings to evaluate where the teams were.

CHAPTER 37

The Mole

Actually, I'm an overnight success. But it took twenty years.
— MONTY HALL

- ♦ What is a "mole" in the upselling process?
- ♦ How can a mole help you sell more in the short term?
- ♦ How can a mole help you sell more in the long term?
- ♦ How can you win a mole to your side?

DURING MY SALES-TRAINING SEMINARS, I always make the point that when you are interviewing during the sales process, it is important to think in the long term and to interview both in terms of the individual and also in terms of the company. Some people think this is just a bit of warm and fuzzy hand-holding that is meant to make our training sound accessible, but it really is a strategically important step to bond with the person as an individual and find out what is going on in his or her world.

I'll tell you why it's so important. If you focus only on corporate initiatives and never focus on the goals and aspirations of the individual, not only will you fail to win the allies who can help you implement your products in the target organization, but you will also miss out on critical information and, ultimately, find yourself subject to the whims of decision makers you never meet.

I also compare the process of finding a corporate ally whom you understand as an individual and as a member of the target company to the process of getting good intelligence. In order to get good information about the enemy, you cannot simply pick up the newspaper and expect to learn what his or her next move is going to be. You have to have a "mole" on the inside. You have to have someone placed within the enemy's headquarters, someone who will keep you informed and give you a heads-up when something big is about to break.

That is exactly what you end up doing when you sell successfully to a single account over a long period of time. By connecting with a decision maker or highly placed insider within the target company and establishing a personal bond with him or her, you not only win a friend, but you also have a mole within the organization. This is absolutely essential if you expect the accounts to grow over time.

Here are some strategies you can use to develop the one-on-one personal relationship necessary to "plant" a mole within the target company.

As a practical matter, in larger accounts, you should probably resign yourself to the fact that a lot of decision making is going to happen independent of your efforts to influence the decision. In other words, the larger the organization, the more likely that intelligence is going to be important for you to position yourself within that account.

What this means, in the real world, is that you'll be in a better position to upsell within that account if you have accurate information about what's actually taking place within the company. This can be, as experience has shown, extremely difficult to track down. The best advice I can give you is, build meaningful relationships with as many people as possible, and make as many people as possible look good.

What we're really talking about is the task of building alliances with people—with at least one and preferably more than one—who can act as moles for you within the organization. I'm not going to kid you. At very large companies, you really do need someone, or a series of someones, who has heard the latest scuttlebutt and who is willing to share it with you. We live in the "information age," so it should not come as a huge surprise to you that your upselling efforts will benefit by gathering as much information as possible from as many different people as possible.

It follows, then, that your goal should be to build up a network, informal but meaningful, with as many people who are friendly or even neutral to your cause as you possibly can. Here are a couple of good ways to build up that kind of a relationship. You can use these strategies for building up your intelligence within the company—for creating moles in your network, people who will tell you what's really going on, at least from their perspective.

Strategy #1

When I get a call from headhunters, and I frequently do, I reach out to my key contacts at my best accounts and say, "Hey, listen, I just got a weird thing, would you call me back?" Inevitably, they call me back. Then I say, "Here's the thing. I got a call from a headhunter. I don't know if this is appropriate for you, or if you know anybody, or if you're looking—I don't know. It's none of my business. But if you are interested, this is a number, this is the situation. Here's the opportunity. Here's the phone number. Mention my name if you call them. I just thought you'd like to know." Suddenly, I'm a guy who's now connecting with you on a more personal level. And you're more likely to share information with me about what's happening in your world.

Strategy #2

Our company subscribes to an editorial service—we get leads via e-mail that tell us which editors want to do which stories and what kinds of experts they're looking for. Some of the leads are appropriate to our business, but most of them aren't. So when I see a lead that seems right for one of my customers, I pass it on. I e-mail the person, and then I follow up with a phone call. I say, "Listen, there's an article here. I subscribe to this service. They're looking for an expert in such-and-such an area. It occurred to me that you might be that expert. You might want to respond to article number two." Again, when you get that kind of call from me, you're more likely to share information that *you* come across.

The principle is startlingly simple. Find a way to do something for someone else, and you'll eventually find that there's a pretty good likelihood that they'll do something for you at some point down the line. I think it was Benjamin Franklin who pointed out that the Golden Rule—"Do unto others as you would have them do unto you"—makes excellent business sense and is not merely a religious principle. In this case, the idea is to pass along critical information that you know will benefit your contact in the hope that he or she will pass you similarly critical information when it comes his or her way. It works!

And guess what? When your mole leaves company A to start a new job at company B, you've got a hot new prospect to call!

| CHAPTER 38 |

"I've Got an Idea. . . ."

Intellectuals solve problems; geniuses prevent them.
—ALBERT EINSTEIN

♦ How can we use creativity to build and strengthen bridges with key contacts within the customer's organization?
♦ How can we move up the pyramid by sharing our ideas?
♦ What does the strategic partner sound like?
♦ How can we involve the CEO of our customer's organization in our upselling initiatives?
♦ How can we win the CEO's help in moving the sale forward?

RECENTLY, I HAD A MEETING with a senior sales executive who works for one of the world's largest manufacturers of industrial chemicals. His main customer was a major global manufacturing company in a fairly heavy industry that is one of the largest producers of engines, trucks, tractors, and so on. The senior VP is getting ready for a meeting with his contact at this heavy equipment manufacturer. So I asked him, "What are you trying to accomplish at this meeting?"

And the sales executive says to me, "Well, I'm always looking for ways to build new products into their order. I'm trying to upsell."

He already has a relationship with this manufacturer, and he would like them to use more of his products. It is only logical he would want to develop an expanded relationship. So I said, "How are you planning on doing that? What are you going to do to expand the relationship?"

And the senior executive says to me, without batting an eye, "Well, I am going to go talk about product X, product Y, and product Z and show them all the specifics on how those products work. I'm going to give him the complete technical breakdown."

I just stopped and stared at him. He had made the classic sales mistake in that he was planning to build his meeting around the idea of executing what we call a "products dump" on his contacts. That means reciting a long litany of technical details or advertising copy and pretending it's a conversation with a customer.

Now, in my sales training programs, I warn people *not* to simply recite the contents of their brochure to a new prospect, *not* to deliver a monologue about all the technical specifications of their product, *not* to go off on a tangent about their own internal quality control program and all the similar programs. I warn people not to do this because it is a great way to turn people off and destroy the rapport of an initial meeting. And, here is a senior executive at one of the largest chemical products manufacturers in the world, planning on taking this exact same approach with a current customer—one who represents literally millions of dollars in sales!

I said, "Let me ask you something. Have you ever once gone in with an idea of how he could use one of these lubricants? In other words, not explaining how the lubricant works, but sharing your own thought about how he could use the lubricant to save money, increase his equipment life, and so on?"

"Gee, I never thought about that," he said. "That's a great idea."

Did you notice that, by *sharing* my idea—one that was about sharing ideas—I was able to move up the pyramid with my customer?

You remember the top of that relationship pyramid we looked at? This is what the strategic partnership looks like. The strategic partner is the guy who walks in the door to meet with his key customer and says, "Hey, I have this great idea. It kept me up all last night. I was thinking about your challenges with your equipment and how you need to be able to extend the workable life of it, and I got together with some of my people, and here's what we came up with. Let me know what you think of this."

That's a strategic partner talking!

A strategic partner does *not* sound like this:

"Our model ZGL compound has been tested in sixty-five different regression analyses, with four different quality networks, and has been reinforced with the additive G239, which protects you from poor alignment of Neptune when the Moon is in the Second House. . . ."

Remember, the point is to walk in the door more concerned about the person's challenge than he or she is. The point is to make it clear that you were up all night worrying about this *and that you have an idea* that you are eager to be able to share with this person. That is the key to upselling . . . and, I think, the key to effective selling.

Getting the CEO on Your Side

Let's look now at a fairly complex upselling strategy that makes use of this "I've got an idea" approach. This strategy involves the CEO of a company that is already buying from us.

This is an interesting dynamic, because CEOs tend to have very short attention spans. This means they sometimes evaporate when you don't want them to. Of course, it's all well and good if the CEO calls a meeting, announces that you are the vendor or supplier of choice, and then orders everyone to carry out the details. Unfortunately, this does not happen very often. What is more likely to take place is that you will have an initial contact with a person at the head of the operation, who will then refer you to others with whom you will have to deal for some period of time.

If you are not extremely careful, what happens next is the evaporation problem: The CEO's initial contact with you is the very last you ever hear from the top. Basically, in the "default" setting, the CEO says that what you are proposing sounds interesting and that he would like to consider doing more business with you, but that he needs you to work with people at other levels in the company before finalizing the purchase arrangements. And he then leaves you to the mercy of the rest of the company.

Six months later, nothing has moved forward.

Bad outcome!

The question is, how do we make sure that the CEO continues to work as an effective advocate for us even though he or she has a million other things to look at and is unlikely to try to make a conscious effort to be involved in our sales process? Here's one approach.

My goal in this situation is simply to schedule a series of breakfasts with the CEO. What I have to do is open up a line of communication and keep it open. Think of your contact with the top person as a pierced earlobe. I know that's an odd comparison—but think it through. If you pierce somebody's ear and you don't put an earring in there for a while, it closes up, and the person can't wear an earring. On the other hand, pierced ears that you constantly put earrings into will stay open.

So I want to keep my line of communication open once I establish it with the CEO. And here's how I do it. Immediately after my *first* breakfast meeting with the CEO, I send him an e-mail message right away. And by "right away," I mean, preferably within twelve hours of my face-to-face meeting.

This e-mail says, basically, "Thank you for meeting with me. This is what we talked about. This is what I'm going to think about. This is what I'm going to do. And I am going to contact you from time to time about new ideas that I have, and I hope we can discuss those."

Every time I get a thought now that might conceivably benefit his company, I send him an e-mail—whether he receives it, whether he does anything, whether he replies or not. If I come up with what seems to me like a good idea, I send it along.

My guess is that 70 percent of the e-mails I send to him get forwarded to other people, even if I don't know about it. Then periodically I call him up. Every six weeks or so I check in with him, and I say, "Hey, let's have breakfast again. I have an idea I want to show you"; then I schedule *another* breakfast meeting. And before the breakfast, I e-mail him: "Here's my thoughts about our upcoming breakfast; here's what I'm thinking of talking about."

He may reject my agenda completely, but at least he knows there's a plan. At a minimum, we have breakfast together. In a better scenario, we're talking about something that is of interest to one of us, and in the best-case scenario, we're talking about the things that I wanted to talk about—namely, how my discussions with his people are going.

Now, I don't necessarily have to make the sale through him. I could let him know what's going on with his own organization. I could say to him, "Listen, I've been calling somebody in your company and I just want to let you know what's going on. I call this guy, he talks to me, this other guy's talking to me, while this guy's been holding me up." I don't ask for help directly. But I let him know what I'm up to and where I'm hitting brick walls.

I'm just bringing him up to date. I really don't drop his name in my discussions with his people. But by having regular breakfast meetings with the top guy and by constantly passing along my ideas, I get his insights, his guidance, and, not infrequently, his quiet help in overcoming the obstacles that might otherwise keep us from doing more business together.

CHAPTER 39

Upselling to a Committee

Eighty percent of success is showing up.
—Woody Allen

- What are the challenges of upselling to a committee?
- What are the opportunities?
- What are the most common mistakes, and how can we avoid them?
- How can we keep the committee from dragging out the sales process?
- How should we follow through after the committee meeting?

First, the bad news. If your upselling initiative requires you to make a presentation before a committee, you are already in trouble. Nine times out of ten, a committee will be most comfortable not taking any action whatsoever. It is basically part of their nature for committees to not actually do anything. If you allow nature to take its course, committees will study, discuss, deliberate, and ultimately abstain from taking any kind of meaningful action in a significant number of the cases involving a decision to buy more stuff from you.

That is the bad news. The good news, which a great many salespeople ignore, is that you can, with a great deal of hard work, counteract this tendency toward inaction. In this chapter, we will look at some of the ways you can do that.

Let's look at some of the specific elements that can kill a decision to purchase more products or services from you. First, you can fail to earn a place on the agenda. This is a favorite tactic within the organization that is eager to purchase from another vendor or perhaps simply even not to buy from you, but that does not want to have to navigate a long-drawn-out conflict over the matter. Instead of placing the question of whether to buy more from you on the agenda, it quietly makes sure the question does not show up in the first place. The best way to counteract this problem is to tactfully ask to see a copy of the agenda for the meeting from one or more of your allies in the organization. It is not inconceivable that your ally thinks you are on the agenda, but your enemies have made sure that you are not.

Perhaps more subtle, but just as damaging in a practical sense, is the situation where you are the last item on the agenda or are placed strategically late in the meeting. This is a recipe for being shelved indefinitely, and it requires basically the same strategy as the problem of not being on the agenda at all.

A third reason upselling attempts can die on the vine is the problem of having the materials you need to deliver an effective presentation delivered too late for your meeting. In other words, there is some kind of logistical problem, and the stuff you need to be able to make a great impression simply does not show up or does not work. There is really nothing internally you can do to overcome this problem, except perhaps put everything into a package that you yourself bring to the meeting. But keep reading, as this, too, carries its share of challenges.

When it comes to upselling or any kind of selling to a committee, the real mistake is to imagine that anyone is going to walk into the meeting neutral on the question of whether to buy your product or service. People already have a bias before the meeting even begins, and there are always political issues to take into account. A fair number of people you run into will be opposed to any initiative that person A proposes, simply because their goal in life is to make person A look bad and to frustrate any of his or her initiatives.

So, looking beyond the obvious challenges that await you in preparing for your meeting with the committee, namely, those of agenda placement or lack of materials, there remains a whole category of internal politics and strategic information gathering that can, if you are not careful, eat up a good deal of time. So, please take this piece of advice: Be sure that the opportunity justifies a good deal of upfront work *before* you invest that up-front work. In other words, if you are confident that the resulting outcome is a $2 million piece of business, and you are convinced that you have a realistic fifty-fifty shot at winning that business, go ahead and do everything else that appears in this chapter to win the additional business. On the other hand, if you are not convinced that you have a fifty-fifty shot, or if the deal is not worth the time and effort, then stop here and think about developing additional business with another of your customers.

Still with me? Good. Here are some basic principles to keep in mind when upselling through committees.

Principle #1: *Know the History*

Find out what kind of committee you are dealing with. Is it a standing committee or an ad hoc committee? An ad hoc committee is something that is put together for the sole purpose of resolving a specific problem and may have a different chain of command than a standing committee does. It is common, for instance, for CEOs and other heavyweights to assemble an ad hoc committee and order it to report back with a recommendation. Whatever the situation is, you will need to know. If it is an ad hoc committee, you will quickly become aware of the fact that these people have never worked together. They may not actually be all that good at working together, and they may welcome your help as a facilitator. On the other hand, if it is a standing committee, there are, in all likelihood, already strong group dynamics at work, as well as a record of past decisions and strategies for implementing those decisions. Find out as much as you can about both by appealing to your contacts before the meeting takes place.

Principle #2: *It Is More Important to Know Who Decided Who Would Be on the Committee Than It Is to Know Who to Target on the Committee Itself*

This is a very important concept. Even on a standing committee, the odds are good that someone in the organization with a good deal of clout had the final say on which people would and would not serve on that committee. For instance, if you were contacting my company, you might well find yourself talking to a member of the committee that handles our franchising decisions. But—and here is the key point—your sales cycle would accelerate dramatically if you found out that I was the person who named each of the individuals to the committee! By contacting me directly and convincing me that you are worth talking to, you would very likely get important information and position yourself much more effectively for winning the committee's approval than you would by contacting each of the individual members themselves.

Principle #3: *Ask Intelligent Questions*

If you are invited to make a presentation before the committee, that means, by definition, that you have a "champion." The champion is a person who wants you to make your pitch. It is all very well to receive this information, but just receiving it and then immediately acting on it shows a lack of foresight. Yes, you may receive additional business from this meeting—but why not improve the odds? Get as much information as you can. Ask your champion why he or she is allowing you to come. Ask him or her whether he or she is personally invested in the outcome. And ask him or her for help in setting up the Next Step. Say beforehand to your champion, "Okay, the meeting is this Friday—can you and I schedule a time right now to meet on the following Monday?" This is perhaps the most important question of all to ask your champion. Use this time to connect with your champion and debrief on what really took place after the meeting. After all, it is very unlikely that the decisions will be delivered to you immediately after you make your presentation.

Principle #4: *Find Out the Real Agenda*

With your champion's permission—or, if the meeting is your idea, with the permission of your most important ally—try to do an informal phone survey of all the people who will be on the committee. You might say, "Would you mind if I contacted some of the people who will be in on the meeting just to find out a little bit about what they are looking for?" In the vast majority of cases, your champion or ally will have no problem with this. It is then imperative that you get on the phone and identify, to whatever degree is possible, what each member of the meeting hopes to see from you. Your call will inevitably include some question like the following: "What do you think, Mr. Contact, that the key concerns of the committee members are going to be?"

Notice that you are not asking the committee member what his or her agenda is, only for his or her assessment of how the committee is likely to view the initiative under discussion. You do not want to put somebody on the spot unnecessarily, and asking the question this way will almost always give you whatever information you are likely to get about this person's agenda.

If you follow these first four principles, you will walk in the door and not be a stranger. You may not have succeeded in the goal of building alliances with everyone on the committee, but at least you will not be a complete unknown, and you will have a good sense of what the group dynamics are.

Principle #5: *Focus on "How"*

During the presentation, put the rhetorical focus on the question of *how* you will be doing more business with this company and not on the issue of whether the company will be buying more products and services from you. Make the assumption that the logistics are what you are there to discuss. After all, you are not going to get a decision today anyway, so why not try to set the agenda moving toward the question of how to begin the additional work together?

One final thought on upselling to committees. The ideas in this chapter are likely to be helpful to you if you find yourself in a situation where you are being asked to make the case for expanding the relationship and formalizing the decision to purchase more products and services. However, although this is a common situation, it is not the optimal one.

The optimal situation, which is relatively rare, is that you get someone who is very high-placed in the organization to make your case for you. In other words, if the CEO is willing to spend ten minutes explaining to others why he has decided to buy more widgets from your company, let him or her do that! You should, if possible, ask if this is a realistic option. Unless your champion is very highly placed in the organization and is also extremely enthusiastic about what you are offering, the odds are good that it will not be a realistic option. But over the course of time, you will run into situations where this type of selling can occur. When it happens, make the most of it.

You may want to suggest to your contact that you help out by creating a summary outline of key points—a draft of major issues. This document will help your champion stay focused as he sings your praises and then moves toward the implementation schedule that both you and your champion feel is appropriate.

CHAPTER 40

Know When to Move On

I don't know the key to success, but the key to failure is trying to please everybody.

—BILL COSBY

♦ When is it a mistake to invest time and effort and attention in an upselling initiative?
♦ What is a one-off?
♦ What are the signs that we are still at the bottom of the relationship pyramid—and are unlikely to be able to move upward?

ONE OF THE MOST neglected truths about upselling is that the very best strategy is sometimes to recognize that there is no possibility to expand a relationship with a given customer. That may sound cynical, but it is actually quite optimistic. The point is not to try to find a magic wand that you can wave over every customer and use to expand his or her budget and devote dollars to your company. No such magic wand exists, and you should not waste your time waiting for one.

The trick is to align yourself so well with the interests of your prospects and customers that you learn to develop a sense for whether or not the possibility really exists to expand your relationship in a way that benefits both parties. The last part of that sentence is particularly crucial, so please read it again. Notice that I said that your goal in upselling must be to develop a proposal or initiative that *benefits both parties*!

Inexperienced salespeople sometimes tell me that they do not see any problem in moving somebody from the prospect stage to the customer stage. Let's say they set an appointment with somebody with whom they have done business before. And let's say that they have a new proposal they want to give that former customer to expand or deepen the relationship—to upsell, in other words.

When I ask an inexperienced salesperson about this kind of relationship, I generally do so by posing a question like this one: "So, why do you think they bought from you in the first place? You told me that they placed an order for widgets three months ago. Why do you think they did that?"

I will get any number of responses to this, but with inexperienced salespeople, the sad truth of the matter is that they will very rarely have any idea exactly why the person bought from them in the first place. As a result, their efforts to expand or upsell the relationship are statistically unlikely to bear fruit. It is not impossible that they could get new business from this customer, mind you, but it is, in my experience, unlikely that you will significantly expand a business relationship when you know absolutely nothing about the reason the person bought from you in the first place. You are still at the commodity level of relationship.

We do not like to admit it to ourselves, but a certain percentage of the people who buy from us buy from us at the commodity level. We help them resolve a short-term problem or address a sudden crisis. We are not part of their long-range plans. The first decision is what I like to call a "one-off." That means that the person really is not supposed to buy from us again, and there is very little that we can do to change that. That is not the way it is in all the cases and with all the customers, but it is what we face in a certain percentage of the relationships. And when we do not do any meaningful exploration of the reasons that prompted the person's decision to work with us in the first place, we should not be surprised when we are not able to move the person up to the next level.

Let me give you an example of what I mean. The business I am in, the sales-training business, has a lot of different reasons that motivate people. Sometimes people buy training because they want to hit a certain sales goal and they feel that the tools that their salespeople have are not sufficient for them to do that. Now you might think that a goal like that is the only guiding motivation when it comes to purchasing sales training, but that is not the case at all. Sometimes, believe it or not, the reason people buy training is that they have a certain number of dollars left in their budget and the end of the year is approaching and they want to be absolutely sure that they still get the same amount in their budget for next year, so they want to be sure to spend it—and quickly.

So, the people in a situation where they have come to the conclusion that their sales team is deficient in certain critical sales skills—say, for instance, setting first appointments—have one reason for calling me up and asking if I will train their team. The people who want to get rid of the $X,000 that is sitting in their budget before the clock runs out have a different agenda in calling me up and asking if I will deliver sales training to their team.

Here is the point: I cannot treat the one situation as though it were the other. In other words, I cannot assume that I know that the person who is calling to get rid of the budget dollars has the same motivation or requirement as the person who wants to see measurable increases in first appointments over the next sixty days. They are two totally different situations. And the person who wants to maintain the same budget level next year, and as a result wants to spend money with me right now, is very likely to be what I call a one-off. This is the kind of sale that may, as a statistical fact, simply be a single piece of business. That is not to say that it is impossible that I could not sell this person. It does mean, however, that I am not going to build up the same level of time, energy, and attention after delivering the program as I will with the other person—especially if I continue to get signals that the only reason that person wanted to work with me in the first place was to get rid of the budget money.

The lesson in this: You are, in my experience, much better off focusing your upselling efforts on somebody your gut says is a "high-percentage shot" than you are focusing your upselling efforts on somebody your gut says is a "low-percentage shot."

I know it's more or less impossible to quantify, but it works for me. Some people really are one-offs, and after just a little bit of experience, you learn to recognize who they are. Don't bother investing large amounts of time and energy trying to develop an upselling campaign for them.

CHAPTER 41

The Hallmarks of an Upselling Sales Culture

The very essence of leadership is that you have to have vision. You can't blow an uncertain trumpet.
—THEODORE M. HESBURGH

♦ What are the beliefs that support a healthy upselling sales culture?

THERE ARE, I BELIEVE, thirteen beliefs that support a positive upselling sales culture. They are:

1. *The objective* of each step is to get to the next step.
2. *The definition* of selling is helping people do what they do better.
3. *No one "needs" us* or what we have to offer; if anyone did "need" us, they would have already called us.
4. *Our number one competitor* is the status quo—what the person or organization is already doing.
5. *Sell to the obvious* by asking how and why the person is already doing what he or she is doing.
6. *The sales process* is an extended conversation; we can control the flow of that conversation.
7. *The longer a sale takes* out of its normal sales cycle, the less likely it is to happen.
8. *The key to effective sales* is ratios, not numbers.

9. *All responses* we hear are in kind; all can be anticipated; all are likely to be told in stories.

10. *Seventy-five percent of the work* in the ideal sales process occurs prior to the proposal, or presentation, of your plan.

11. *Our upselling close* should be a natural outgrowth of the sales process that sounds like this: "Makes sense to me—what do you think?"

12. *We want the prospect to decide to buy more from us*; we don't want to have to sell to the prospect.

13. *We can predict future income* based on current activity.

CHAPTER 42

The Shopping Bag Rules

A person is a success if he gets up in the morning and gets to bed at night, and in between he does what he wants to do.
—BOB DYLAN

THE FOLLOWING LIST of twenty-one strategies for true success is not my invention. It was given to me by someone who spotted it on, of all places, the outside of a shopping bag. If there has ever been a less likely medium for the communication of profound, life-changing advice, I have never heard of it. But I do believe that all twenty-one of these pieces of advice will help you to obtain true success in your life, and they will support your objectives professionally and personally. The final piece of upselling advice I have for you in this book is that you upsell yourself by making a commitment to invest in each and every one of the following success principles. Implement each of them to the degree that you are able, and you will see the payoff.

1. Work at something you enjoy . . . something worthy of your own time and talent.
2. Give people more than they expect and do so cheerfully.
3. Become the most positive and enthusiastic person you know.
4. Be forgiving of yourself and others.
5. Be generous.
6. Have a grateful heart.
7. Be persistent. Be persistent. Be persistent.
8. Discipline yourself to save money even on a modest salary.
9. Treat everyone you meet in the way that you would want to be treated.

10. Commit yourself to constant improvement.
11. Commit yourself to quality.
12. Understand that happiness is not based on possessions, power, or prestige, but on relationships with people you love and respect.
13. Be loyal.
14. Be honest.
15. Be a self-starter.
16. Be decisive even if it means you will sometimes be wrong.
17. Stop blaming others. Take responsibility for every area of your life.
18. Be bold and courageous. When you look back on your life, you will regret the things you did not do more than the ones you did.
19. Take good care of those you love.
20. Don't do anything that wouldn't make your mom proud.
21. Act as though your creator were watching. He is.

Customer Service Principles

10 Common Customer Service Obstacles

#1: Customer's Lack of Rapport with Salesperson or Company Representative

- No commonality
- No person-to-person connection
- Conversation sounds precisely the same with this customer as it would with any other customer—same words, intonations, suggestions, etc.

#2: Company's Lack of Accountability

- "It's not my job"—with no attempt to acknowledge company's ultimate responsibility for the problem
- Customer repeats story for second, third, fourth, fifth time to a new person
- Customer never hears "I'm sorry"

#3: Company's Lack of Empathy

- No effort to feel emotions customer is feeling
- No effort to identify with customer situation
- No effort to find out how customer has handled repercussions of problem with friends, loved ones, own customers, etc.

#4: Company's Lack of Respect

- Condescending tone
- Carrying over stress from previous call or customer interaction
- Inappropriate language

#5: No Concern for Customer's Time

- Sending customers to other departments
- Keeping customers on hold
- Making customer start from scratch—start all over either in person or off-site

#6: Escalation

- Raising the tension level in the exchange
- Bullying
- Sarcasm

#7: Disconnect

- Salesperson or customer service representative pretends "I can't hear you"
- Repeats stock response two or more times to customer's question or issue
- Makes customer repeat information he or she has already given

#8: Jargon

- Salesperson or customer service representative uses technical terms customer will not understand
- Uses administrative terms and processes customer will not understand
- Talks in company's language rather than the customer's (The real expert is the one who can make himself understood.)

#9: No Chance for Input

- Salesperson or customer service representative talks too much or too fast
- Assumes this customer has the same precise problem, situation, or reaction as the last customer
- Assumes he/she already knows the relevant solution *or*
- Assumes he/she cannot solve the customer's problem—early attempt to resolve the exchange and move on, without taking part in any meaningful discussion

#10: No Follow-through or Investment in Relationship

- No clear Next Step
- No sense that organization will deliver on direct or indirect commitments
- The "ball" always ends in the customer's court
- No attempt to resolve discussion or problem to customer's satisfaction

10 Proven Principles for Retaining Customers and Winning Add-On Business

1. Establish one-on-one rapport.
2. Be accountable for something.
3. Validate emotions, not content.
4. Show respect and stay poised even when the customer vents.
5. Respect the customer's time.
6. Do not escalate.
7. Never disconnect, but know when and how to disengage.
8. Use terms the customer will understand.
9. Give the customer opportunity for input—and measure the input.
10. Make sure someone follows through.

A Retail Upselling Model

LET ME SHARE WITH YOU a selling model that we use in the retail industry that is devoted to winning sales at the counter . . . *and* to helping win back what is known as a "skip" customer.

A skip customer is someone who buys from you once and then vanishes forever. This kind of customer is particularly sought after for repeat business in the high-end clothing industry. The goal is, of course, once we get someone to decide that it makes sense to purchase a suit from us for $650, to be sure that the next time that person buys a suit, he or she will walk into our store, and not any other store, to make his or her next clothing purchase.

This, however, is much more easily said than done. The problem is that we can have a great relationship, deliver a great product, and even help the person conclude that the product is exactly the type that he or she would like to see more of—but if we do not maintain the relationship over time with the customer, what we are going to find is that these people continue to drop off the radar screen.

Sometimes they will drop off our radar screen because they simply do not remember where they bought the suit! Other times, they will drop off the map because it has been so long since they heard from us that they will assume that we have gone out of business or that there has been some other type of problem on our end (indifference is a great killer of sales of upselling revenue).

It is even possible that people might drop off of our map because they heard something inaccurate about us from the competition! Since we are not in an ongoing communication relationship with the customer, we have no way to counteract what our competitors are saying.

Take a look at the following model, which we used to train people in the retail-clothing sector to use when interacting with potential customers.

Step #1

The first step is *engagement*. We approach the customer and make him or her feel at home.

Step #2

The second step is to use questions to *gauge* the person's level of interest and find out what's happening in his or her life. After we have established some kind of meaningful rapport with the person, we may pay a (believable!) compliment and/or ask appropriate questions. These are usually questions that help to elicit what has changed in the person's life enough to make him or her decide to walk into the store. We also want to know when, how, and why the person bought a similar item the last time around. Is this piece of clothing being purchased for a special occasion? Is it something that is going to be worn to work every day? Is it a continuation of an existing look? Is this piece of clothing meant to mark a psychological dividing point in the person's life—after a divorce, say? These are the kinds of questions that it is good to have some kind of answer to. We may not be able to ask for all of the details in precisely the way that we want, but we can certainly find out what brought the person into the store, what has changed in his or her world, and how the last purchase was undertaken.

Whatever reason your customer has for purchasing clothing in the manner he or she is doing, we want to be able to offer up confirming reasons from your own experience or those of your customer base. So, if the person is saying, "I am buying this suit for a Bar Mitzvah," you can respond by answering that there are a lot of people who come to your shop because they are getting ready for Bar Mitzvahs. You might even share a couple of anecdotes from your own experience about people who have had recent Bar Mitzvahs or who have prepared for Bar Mitzvahs who are customers of yours.

Step #3

The next step is to *show* the person something relevant to his or her world. Notice that, up to this point, we really have made no effort whatsoever to make any kind of recommendation to the person. We have not come on strong, nor have we uttered the dreaded words that retail customers around the country, and indeed the world, have learned to dread: "How can I help you today?"

Instead, what we have done is built up some information and confirmed the reasons behind the person's visit to the store. It is only at this point that we will continue the conversation by saying something along the lines of, "You've got to see this . . ." What we point the customer to at that moment, we hope, will match up with a concern, objective, or driving goal that has something to do with the reason he or she has stepped into the store in the first place.

We continue this process, repeating Steps 2 and 3 as long as it feels comfortable to do so. That means we may ask a lot of questions and show off a lot of stuff. In this situation, the *longer* the conversation goes, the more favorable it is to the seller. (Outside of the retail setting—specifically during a prospecting telephone call, where our goal is simply to set up a face-to-face meeting—the long conversation is not to the seller's advantage.)

Now, up to this point, you may be thinking to yourself, this model is not really about upselling at all. All we have done is help the person connect with the right suit of clothes. Look how we move forward, though.

Once we *show* something, or perhaps a series of somethings, by using a phrase like "You've got to see this . . ." or "I want to show you something . . . ," the customer is eventually going to reach a decision. Maybe that decision will be to buy from us that day, and maybe it won't. We certainly hope that it will be a decision to buy from us!

But whether that person decides to buy from us that day or not, we are going to set up a plan that follows through on the final step of the model, *following through.* We are going to find a way to stay in touch. We are going to ask the person for his or her contact information, ideally an e-mail address. We are going to set up some kind of Next Step, perhaps a special that we would like the person to be able to take a look at or even an invitation to an event off-site. It does not really matter what kind of Next Step we come up with—it could be as simple as a telephone call to let the person know when a new style or product has come in—but we do need to try and get something on the radar screen, and possibly for at some point within the next two weeks. I do recommend that we try and reestablish contact with this customer for some point within the next two weeks, at least for the first contact period.

Why am I emphasizing this staying in touch strategy so heavily? Because we want to build a relationship with this person. We want to make sure this person gets an invitation to our next event or sale. We want to make sure he or she gets our company newsletter. We want to be able to call this person to let him or her know that something interesting has arrived.

In fact, we want this person to begin to think of us a little bit less like a store he might wander into, and a little bit more like a retail consultant who is working at no charge. Such a consultant will keep in touch and offer insights and suggestions that are relevant to the customer's situation. If the customer did not buy from us during that first trip to the store, we want to keep him or her apprised of all the new developments and all the new merchandise. If the customer did buy from us during the first visit, we want to make sure that that first visit is not the last. Our aim is to establish a relationship and to find some way to encourage the customer to think of it as a relationship, as well.

Once we do that, we will find that the statistical likelihood of additional purchases from this customer will grow dramatically.

A Compressed Approach

Let me tell you my favorite approach to selling—and upselling—in the retail environment.

What typically happens when you walk into a store? I have already alluded to this briefly: The salesperson either ignores you or pounces on you, forcing a showdown with the words, "How can I help you?" or some variation. We all know these words are coming, and we all expect them. So when they actually do come, they have no real effect, other than raising and heightening our defenses. But there is a different way to sell—and upsell—in the retail selling environment, and I want to share it with you here.

Suppose you were to walk into the retail store of your choice, and instead of being badgered or ignored, you got a couple of minutes to look around. And suppose, after you'd looked around a little, you noticed someone walking your way with a smile on his or her face. The person is respecting your time, your intellect, and your physical space. Before you have the chance to be taken aback, and in a very gentle tone of voice, the person simply says to you, "Did you see anything you absolutely, positively can't live without?"

The humor is slightly self-defacing, as though the retail salesperson knows full well that you are not making a decision on his or her timetable, but rather on yours. So you smile back at the person, who seems very pleasant, and answer, "No, not really."

Then the retail salesperson nods briefly, as though confirming the suspicion that this would be your answer, and then you notice something odd. The retail salesperson's eyes twinkle just a little bit. You see a hand beckoning toward you, urging you to approach.

"I thought so," says the salesperson. "Let me show you something really remarkable."

Who on earth is not going to be interested in seeing something really remarkable? Especially when the proposition is laid out in such a nonthreatening and almost self-critical way. The body language, the opening remarks, and everything else indicate that this is a person who really is not interested in overpowering you or forcing you to make a choice, but instead simply interested in sharing something extraordinary with you.

Index

About the Author

STEPHAN SCHIFFMAN is president of D.E.I. Management Group, Inc., one of the largest sales-training companies in the United States. He is the author of a number of best-selling books, including *Cold Calling Techniques (That Really Work!)*; *Power Sales Presentations*; *The 25 Most Common Sales Mistakes*; *The 25 Habits of Highly Successful Salespeople*; *Asking Questions, Winning Sales*; *Make It Happen Before Lunch*; *25 Sales Skills They Don't Teach at Business School*; *Getting to "Closed"*; *Telesales*; *Closing Techniques* (3rd edition); and most recently, *25 Most Dangerous Sales Myths and How to Avoid Them*. Schiffman's articles have appeared in *The Wall Street Journal*, *The New York Times*, and *INC.* magazine. He has also appeared as a guest on CNBC's *Minding Your Business*, *How to Succeed in Business*, and *Smart Money*. For more information about Stephan Schiffman and D.E.I. Management, visit *www.dei-sales.com*.

About D.E.I. Management Group

D.E.I. MANAGEMENT GROUP, INC., founded in 1979 by Stephan Schiffman, has long been recognized as one of the nation's premier sales-training companies, delivering skills and management programs for organizations ranging from Fortune 500 companies to startups.

Using face-to-face training and distance-learning programs, we help organizations better do what they do, by effecting measurable improvements in the most critical aspects of the sales process:

- Effective prospecting
- Efficient execution of the sales process (face-to-face and tele-phone)
- Productive management of prospecting and selling activity

To date, we have trained over half a million salespeople in North America, South America, Europe, and Asia at more than 9,000 companies, including Nextel Communications, Boise Office Solutions, Cox Communications, Fleet Bank, and Datamonitor . . . to name a few.

Franchising Opportunities with America's Premier Sales-Training Firm
If you are a . . .

Self-starter
With sales experience
And the desire to succeed and gain financial freedom

. . . then D.E.I. offers you an exciting business opportunity—the chance to own your own firm in the vitally important sales-training industry, while enjoying the benefits of an outstanding franchising company with a superior selling system.

We're looking to award franchises to a select group of qualified, self-motivated individuals who are willing to follow a proven system for success. You might be one of them.

Visit *www.dei-sales.com* for more information!

Practical and proven strategies
from America's #1 Sales Trainer!

Schiffman's *25 Sales* Series
Everything they didn't teach you in business school!

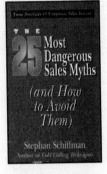
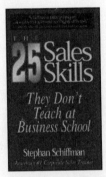